BODY 2.0

THE ENGINEERING REVOLUTION IN MEDICINE

SARA LATTA

TWENTY-FIRST CENTURY BOOKS / MINNEAPOLIS

Many thanks to my editor par excellence,
Domenica Di Piazza, whose intellectual
curiosity, editorial rigor, and boundless
patience made this book what it is

Twenty-First Century Books
An imprint of Lerner Publishing Group, Inc.
241 First Avenue North
Minneapolis, MN 55401 USA

For reading levels and more information, look up this title
at www.lernerbooks.com.

Main body text set in Conduit ITC Std.
Typeface provided by International Typeface Corp.

Library of Congress Cataloging-in-Publication Data

Names: Latta, Sara L., author.
Title: Body 2.0 : the engineering revolution in medicine / Sara Latta.
Description: Minneapolis : Twenty-First Century Books, [2020] | Audience: Age
    13–18. | Audience: Grade 9 to 12. | Includes bibliographical references and
    index. |
Identifiers: LCCN 2018054864 (print) | LCCN 2018056397 (ebook) |
    ISBN 9781541543904 (eb pdf) | ISBN 9781541528130 (lb : alk. paper)
Subjects: LCSH: Biomedical engineering—Juvenile literature. | Regeneration
    (Biology)—Juvenile literature.
Classification: LCC R856.2 (ebook) | LCC R856.2 .L38 2020 (print) |
    DDC 610.28—dc23

LC record available at https://lccn.loc.gov/2018054864

Manufactured in the United States of America
1-44689-35528-5/2/2019

CONTENTS

INTRODUCTION

FROM WOODEN TOES TO BIOBOTS

Biomedical engineering isn't exactly new. Humankind has been tinkering with ways to supplement, repair, or replace body parts for thousands of years. The oldest known prosthesis, a wooden toe, was found on an ancient Egyptian mummy. Contact lenses, eyeglasses, and hearing aids are commonplace in the twenty-first century. They are all examples of the ways in which we use biomedical engineering to modify our bodies in response to injury or disease. We are in the midst of a revolution in biomedical engineering that will forever change the way we think about medicine and maybe even life itself.

With new technologies, we can grow new organs or tissues in the lab, using a patient's own cells, to replace or repair diseased or damaged organs. Tiny organs-on-a-chip may soon become important methods of testing the effects of drugs on individual patients. We have tools to edit and correct defective

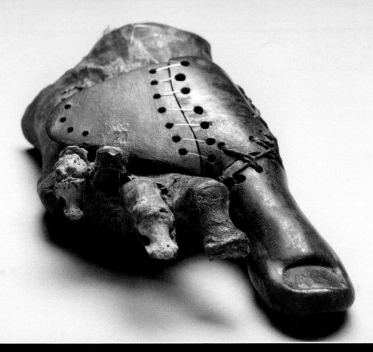

In 2017 archaeologists discovered this prosthetic toe in an ancient Egyptian grave site. The wooden prosthesis is at least three thousand years old—one of the oldest ever found—and was attached to a female mummy, which researchers determined was that of a priest's daughter.

genes in the bodies of people with inherited diseases with a precision never before possible.

Neuroengineers, or engineers who use principles and techniques to study and treat disorders or injuries to the nervous system, have new tools and technologies to tap into the nervous system's capabilities. With brain-computer interfaces (BCIs), people who are paralyzed can use robotic arms, or even their own arms, just by thinking about it. Artificial retinas may soon give blind people new sight. The retina is the layer of nerve cells lining the back wall inside the eye that senses light and sends signals to the brain. Scientists are learning how to control neural, or brain, circuits with light.

In his famous work "Song of Myself," nineteenth-century American poet Walt Whitman wrote, "I am large, I contain multitudes." Although he was referring to the complex and often contradictory nature of individuals, little did he know that humans have multitudes of microbes (bacteria and other microorganisms)—trillions of them, mostly in our digestive tract. Humans have one hundred times as many microbial genes than human genes inside their bodies.

The microbiota, our body's constellation of microbes, plays a vital role in human health and disease. Bioengineering applies engineering principles of design and analysis to studying biological systems and developing biomedical technology. Bioengineers are using the human microbiome to fight obesity, diseases of the immune system, cancer, and mental illness. We may soon enlist microbes, including some of the trillions living inside our bodies, to help us fight cancer and other diseases, or use biobots (robots that are partly or totally made of biological materials) to deliver drugs to specific cells.

Biomedical engineering is nothing more than applying the principles and problem-solving techniques of engineering to biology and medicine. Nothing more, and yet it's fueling a revolution in medicine.

IF A SALAMANDER CAN GROW A NEW LEG, WHY CAN'T I?

I n 1768 the Italian scientist Lazzaro Spallanzani reported that certain worms, snails, and amphibians had the remarkable capacity to regenerate, or regrow, amputated body parts. He could chop off the leg of a salamander, and—voila!— it would grow back again. His claim that snails could sometimes even grow a new head caught the attention of Voltaire, a French writer and philosopher. Voltaire successfully repeated the experiment and wrote a letter to a friend expressing his hope that humans would one day be able to harness the ability to regrow body parts. He added, with his characteristic wit, that for many people a different head might be a great improvement.

The reality of humans growing new heads is perhaps ludicrous. But advances in medicine and bioengineering have moved regeneration in humans from the realm of science fiction toward reality.

Scientists such as Karen Echeverri at the Marine Biological Laboratory in Woods Hole, Massachusetts, are studying axolotls (*above*) to learn more about how this vertebrate (animal with a spinal column) regenerates body parts and organs. Sea stars (*below*), also known as starfish, are invertebrates that are closely related to sea urchins and sand dollars. Scientists have identified about two thousand species of sea star in the world's oceans. Five-arm varieties like this one are the most common, but some species have ten, twenty, and even forty arms. Sea stars can regenerate their arms and body organs.

Humans *do* have a limited capacity for regeneration. We regenerate the top layer of our skin, or epidermis, every two weeks. We can regrow our liver from as little as one-quarter of its original mass. Children up to the age of fifteen who have lost a fingertip can sometimes regenerate a new one, as long as there is a bit of fingernail left and the wound isn't stitched up. But unlike salamanders, starfish, and snails, we can't grow an entire limb or an organ—not yet, anyway. To understand why not and how scientists are trying to figure out how to re-create that secret sauce of regeneration for humans, we need to understand how we generate new cell types.

STEM CELLS 101

The human body has more than two hundred types of cells. Most of them are highly specialized to carry out specific functions. Neurons, or nerve cells, transmit information from the brain to different parts of the body. Muscle cells create movement. Blood cells carry oxygen from the lungs to the heart and brain, and those same cells combat disease. Skin cells protect our internal organs from harm from the outside world. You would no more ask a skin cell to carry out the task of a blood cell than you would ask your dentist to repair your car (assuming your dentist is not also a skilled mechanic).

But the human stem cell has the superhero-like power to transform itself into all other types of cells. It's what gives fetuses in the womb the ability to grow a whole body from scratch. After a sperm fertilizes an egg cell, it divides again and again, becoming a hollow ball of embryonic stem cells. Those multitalented stem cells continue to divide, with each new cell having the potential to either remain a stem cell or, given the right chemical signal, to become a nerve cell, muscle cell, or any other cell type. Nine months later, that five-day-old ball of stem cells—about the size of the period at the end of this sentence—is born, transformed into a squirming little bundle of joy. The scientific term for the embryonic stem cell's ability to transform itself into all manner of cell types is pluripotency.

Scientists in the lab use human embryonic stem cells for research. All these cells came from embryos that develop from eggs through in vitro

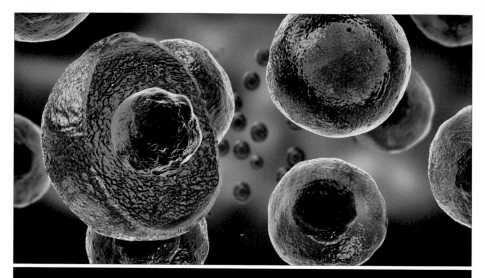

Scientists use embryonic stem cells (*3D illustration above*) in their research. These cells are pluripotent. They can develop into any type of cell in the body.

fertilization. Couples who cannot get pregnant through sexual reproduction sometimes go to an in vitro fertilization clinic. They donate eggs and sperm, which technicians join in the laboratory. This usually results in more embryos than can be used for a pregnancy, so the couples might voluntarily donate extra embryos to research labs.

Embryonic stem cells exist only at the earliest stages of development. Tissue-specific stem cells—sometimes called adult stem cells—appear later in development. They're not quite as versatile as embryonic stem cells, but they're essential players. Adult stem cells are multipotent, and they do the job of creating a small number of new types of cells to perform specific tasks. Most of our body cells wear out over time, and some cells are lost because of injury or disease. The body needs to replace them. Our hardworking skin cells, for example, last a little less than a month before they are replaced by new skin cells. Red blood cells are good for about 115 days. The human body is continually in need of new cells.

Adult stem cells generally reside in the organ or tissue that they serve. Human bone marrow, for example, contains stem cells that form all the types of blood cells in the body—red and white blood cells, as well as platelets (the blood cells responsible for blood clotting). Skin stem cells live in the deepest, or innermost, layer of the epidermis.

When it comes to using stem cells for research and medical treatment, embryonic stem cells might seem to be ideal. They are easy to isolate from embryos, and they grow and reproduce well in petri dishes in the lab. They can be cloned to make many exact copies of the original stem cell. Scientists can use them to create stem cell lines—a group of identical stem cells—that researchers can grow indefinitely in the lab or freeze and then thaw for future use. (Scientists in the United States have access to 398 human stem cell lines approved for government-funded research.) By changing the conditions in the culture dish, scientists can coax embryonic stem cells into morphing into tissue-specific cells—muscle, nerve, or whatever is needed.

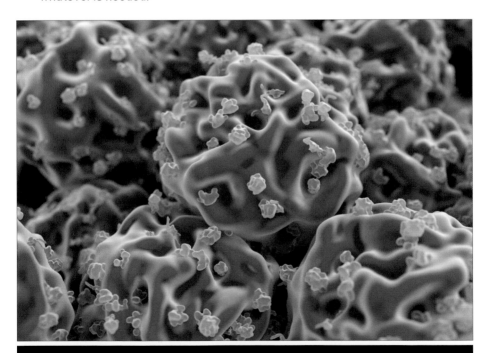

Adult stem cells are found in tissues or organs and can develop into some or all of the major specialized cell types of that tissue or organ.

Adult stem cells are less plentiful in tissues and difficult to isolate. Scientists also have more difficulty getting them to grow and reproduce in the lab. And naturally occurring adult stem cells can only renew themselves or the specialized stem cells of a particular tissue or organ.

For all the limitations of adult stem cells, researchers prefer to use them. For one thing, embryonic stem cells carry a great deal of ethical baggage. For those who believe life begins at conception, the embryo is a human life and destroying it would be wrong. And because embryonic stem cells come from a specific human donor with a unique immune system, the recipient's immune system may reject it. Scientists are working on methods to overcome this problem.

A huge breakthrough for tissue engineering came in 2006. Japanese scientist Shinya Yamanaka had developed a new type of stem cell that could be reprogrammed. In 2006 he took skin cells from adult mice and infected them with a virus that could introduce genes from mice embryo cells into another mouse. The infected skin cells looked and acted just like embryonic stem cells, with the ability to develop into any kind of cell type. A year later, scientists at the University of Wisconsin–Madison did the same thing with human cells from a donor. Yamanaka was one of two people awarded the Nobel Prize in Physiology or Medicine in 2012 for the discovery that adult stem cells can be reprogrammed to become pluripotent. These new cells are induced pluripotent stem cells (iPS cells).

Shinya Yamanaka (*left*) received a Nobel Prize in Physiology or Medicine in 2012 for his work on iPS cells. In this photo, India's Prime Minister Shri Narendra Modi (*right*) shakes hands with Yamanaka during a visit to the Center for iPS Cell Research and Application at Kyoto University in Japan, on August 31, 2014.

DNA DOUBLE HELIX

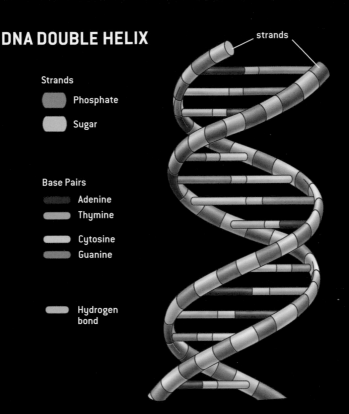

strands

Strands

Phosphate

Sugar

Base Pairs

Adenine

Thymine

Cytosine

Guanine

Hydrogen
bond

DNA is a molecule that contains the instructions a living thing needs to develop, live, and reproduce. These instructions are contained inside every cell. DNA is made of molecules called nucleotides: adenine (A), thymine (T), guanine (G), and cytosine (C). A, T, G, and C are like the alphabet used to write the operating instructions of the cell. The DNA molecules are packaged into threadlike structures called chromosomes.

It might seem that iPS cells are the perfect alternative to embryonic or adult stem cells for regenerative medicine. In this type of medicine, scientists and doctors could take a person's skin or blood cells, turn them into iPS cells, and use them to grow new liver cells, muscle cells, or whatever is needed to treat a condition or a disease. Patients would not face the risk of rejection or the ethical concerns of using embryonic stem cells.

SHADY STEM CELL CLINICS

Stem cell research and regenerative medicine hold a great deal of potential, although in many cases effective therapies are still years away. In recent years, however, at least six hundred unlicensed clinics in the United States alone have begun selling unproven stem cell treatments to desperate patients with conditions ranging from autism to spinal cord injuries. The clinics isolate adult stem cells from patients—with their consent, and usually from belly fat—and inject them back into specific sites in the patient. The claim is that the stem cells can replace or heal damaged tissue, even though no clinical trials back up that claim.

While websites for the stem cell clinics feature testimonials from satisfied customers, the treatments are at best a waste of money. The cost of the treatments, which can be in the thousands of dollars, are not covered by insurance. Worse, they may be dangerous. At least four people have gone blind or suffered severe eye damage from stem cell injections at unlicensed clinics.

Critics of these unlicensed stem cell clinics have called them "medicine's Wild West" and pushed for more regulation. Defenders of the clinics argue that using a patient's own stem cells doesn't qualify as a new drug therapy, so the treatments shouldn't have to go through the long and expensive process required of new drugs. And, they say, people should have the right to try out untested therapies if they want to.

Medicine's Wild West may be ending. In 2018 the US Food and Drug Administration (FDA), the agency that approves new drugs, filed federal complaints. The documents seek to ban two clinics from marketing stem cell therapies without government approval.

Although iPS cells hold a great deal of promise, progress in creating personalized iPS cells for regenerative medicine has been slow. The iPS cells that come from adult stem cells come from living humans. During their

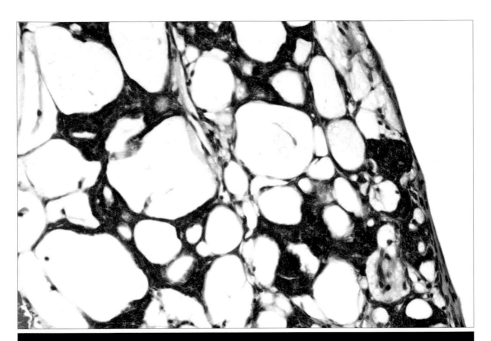

Blastemas, like the ones shown in this colorized micrograph, are groups of stem cells capable of regenerating new tissues or organs.

lives, the human donors have been exposed to a variety of environmental toxins and sunlight that can damage cellular deoxyribonucleic acid (DNA, the material that carries genetic information). Scientists worry that iPS cells could therefore mutate, or change, at some point into potential cancer cells. Although scientists can reprogram a patient's cells, it is expensive to do so and to treat that patient with their own reprogrammed cells. Scientists may well overcome those hurdles. Meanwhile, iPS cells have become an important tool for testing drugs in the lab and studying diseases.

SECRETS OF THE AXOLOTL

With three feathery branches (actually external gills) on either side of its head and a permanently goofy smile, the axolotl is an intriguing creature. But that's not why scientists like Karen Echeverri, associate scientist at the Eugene Bell Center for Regenerative Biology and Tissue Engineering at the Marine Biological Laboratory, Woods Hole, Massachusetts, are

RACKED! HOW DEER REGENERATE ANTLERS

Axolotls may be the champions of regeneration, but one mammal regenerates a new organ every year—a trick that no other mammal can pull off. Every spring, male deer (a family that includes elk, moose, reindeer, and the familiar white-tailed deer) begin to sprout antlers from their foreheads. From spring until fall, a layer of fuzzy skin called velvet covers the buck's antlers. Blood vessels and nerves surround the rapidly developing bone within. And the development *is* rapid: a 441-pound (200 kg) red deer may grow antlers weighing as much as 66 pounds (30 kg) in just three months. That comes out to about three-quarters of an inch (2 cm) a day!

When the velvet begins to shrink and die in the fall, the buck rubs his antlers on trees until only exposed antler bones are left. He will use these weapons to fight other males during mating season. When he has no more use for the antlers, they fall off—and the cycle begins again the next spring.

The remarkable thing is that antlers, unlike the horns of rhinos or cattle, are actual organs. The proliferating cells that divide and grow to make the new antler form a blastema, much like that of the axolotl. The question on some scientists' minds is whether humans can learn from deer—mammals like us—how to regenerate new organs.

In the spring each year, deer such as this white-tailed buck sprout velvet-covered antlers.

so intrigued by the Mexican salamander. Axolotls are "champions of regeneration," says Echeverri. They may be able to teach us how to regenerate our own limbs.

Not only can the axolotl regenerate an amputated tail or leg, it can regrow a severed spinal cord, a damaged brain, or a heart. Every tissue— bone, nerve, muscle, and skin—is replaced with full functionality and without a bit of scarring.

When an axolotl's limb is amputated, a clot of blood cells immediately forms to stop the bleeding at the site. A layer of cells quickly grows to cover the wound site. Over the next few days, a blastema begins to form. Blastemas are made of satellite cells—stem cells for muscle, bone, and other dividing cells that will contribute to regenerating all the different tissue types in the limb. They quickly grow and divide. Echeverri says that humans also have satellite cells, although we run out of them as we age. But axolotls never seem to run out of them.

"When we take a look at the axolotl's genes [the ones that regulate regeneration]," Echeverri said, "we see that they're highly similar to our genes. That suggests that when we get an initial injury, our genes react differently." Rather than growing a new limb, our genes tell the body to form scar tissue to prevent further injury and infections. "We [researchers] think that, for example, if we can intervene very quickly after a spinal cord injury, we might be able to . . . direct those [local] cells toward a pro-regenerative response, instead of [a] scar tissue response."

ORGANS MADE
TO ORDER

Luke Massella was born with spina bifida, a birth
defect in which the backbone that protects the
spinal cord doesn't form to close over and cover that
part of the body. The result is often damage to the
spinal cord and nerves. Like many children with the
defect, the boy's spinal cord nerves that control
the bladder didn't work properly. Children with the
condition are frequently unable to control their
bladder. Because Luke couldn't empty his bladder on
his own, urine would often back up into his kidneys, a
complication that can cause serious kidney damage.
The only solution was to drain his bladder with a
catheter (a narrow tube inserted into the urethra)
several times a day. By the time Luke was ten years
old, even frequent catheterization was no longer
working. His kidneys were failing, no longer able to
remove waste, salt, and extra water from his body.
His energy level was so low he could no longer get
out of bed to go to school.

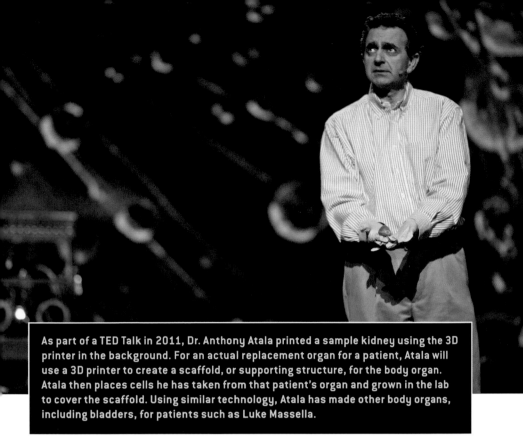

As part of a TED Talk in 2011, Dr. Anthony Atala printed a sample kidney using the 3D printer in the background. For an actual replacement organ for a patient, Atala will use a 3D printer to create a scaffold, or supporting structure, for the body organ. Atala then places cells he has taken from that patient's organ and grown in the lab to cover the scaffold. Using similar technology, Atala has made other body organs, including bladders, for patients such as Luke Massella.

A kidney transplant wasn't an option because even with a new kidney, Luke would still have the same malfunctioning bladder that caused the problem. He could go on dialysis, an ongoing, costly, and time-consuming procedure to clean the blood. Doctors could repair his bladder with tissue from his own intestines. This one-hundred-year-old procedure creates new bladders for patients with bladder cancer. But that wasn't a great option, especially for a boy as young as Luke was. The intestine is designed to absorb fluids, while the bladder holds in fluids. Luke's "leaky" intestinal tissue could potentially lead to other illnesses, including cancer.

In 1999 Luke's parents decided to try a still-experimental surgery offered by Anthony Atala. The young physician at Boston Children's Hospital in Massachusetts was also a research fellow at Harvard Medical School. Atala, now the director of the Institute for Regenerative Medicine at Wake Forest University in Winston-Salem, North Carolina, had seen too many young people die waiting months or years for a desperately needed replacement organ. Those who did get kidney or liver transplants often had serious immune responses—including rejection—to the transplanted organ. Atala believed that a better way was to use the patient's own cells to grow a new organ in the lab and then surgically implant it into the body. "It sounded very science-fictiony at the time," he told *Scientific American,* "but I was certain that it was the future."

So Atala built replacement bladders for Luke and six other children with spina bifida. He used collagen—the most abundant protein in the body and one of the building blocks that holds tissues together—and a synthetic polymer (a compound with repeating units) to create a balloon-shaped scaffold, about the size of a baseball. He took samples of the smooth muscle cells on the outside of Luke's bladder. He also took samples of the epithelial cells that line the inner walls of the bladder. He then grew them separately in a cell culture. Atala knew that mature cells like Luke's lost the ability to expand—divide and multiply—in the lab. Atala came up with a protocol, or method, that allowed him to take a 0.4-inch (1 cm) specimen and expand it so that it would cover an entire football field in just eight weeks! Getting the cells to divide and multiply into usable amounts was a remarkable accomplishment.

When he had enough of each type of cell, Atala coated the insides of the scaffold with bladder cells and the outsides with muscle cells. He allowed the cells to grow on the scaffold in a soup of nutrients for several weeks. Then a team of surgeons sewed the new bladder to Luke's own bladder, increasing his body's ability to hold urine. In surgery Atala wrapped the new bladder with omentum, a tissue rich in blood vessels, so that the bladder cells would receive key nutrients and oxygen throughout Luke's life.

The experiment was a success. Because of his nerve damage, Luke still needed to use a catheter to empty his bladder, but his quality of life was greatly improved. The extra bladder capacity meant that the pressure on his kidneys decreased, and he didn't have to worry about leaking urine.

He gained back his strength and was able to play baseball. In high school, he became the captain of his wrestling team. Luke went on to college, graduating from the University of Connecticut in 2013. "I'll always have spina bifida," he told *UConn Magazine*, "but I'm totally happy with where I am. I'm thankful not only that I'm able to walk, but also play sports. I can now live close to a normal life."

Luke and the other six children to receive the replacement bladders were the first human recipients of lab-grown organs. Since then Atala and others have created and implanted other tissues—small arteries, skin, and even a full trachea, or windpipe. Creating more complex organs such as hearts, lungs, or kidneys poses an even greater challenge. With solid organs like these, it's not just a matter of creating spherical or cylindrical scaffolds and seeding cells onto them, as Atala did when building bladders. These organs are architecturally complex and are made of many different cell types. They require an extensive network of blood vessels.

The solution may lie in an approach that Atala and other researchers are developing using 3D printers. The process starts with creating a 3D blueprint of the object using computer-aided design (CAD) software. Regular inkjet printers lay down a single layer of ink on a two-dimensional surface. But 3D printers follow the CAD software instructions to lay down many thin layers of a material in succession. People are already using this type of printing to create objects ranging from auto parts to jewelry, using materials such as plastic, stainless steel, and even chocolate as their "ink." Why not print using living cells?

Atala's team has developed a 3D bioprinter to create a human jawbone, muscle, and even an ear. To create the ear, the team took a computerized tomography (CT) scan of a human ear and used that series of X-rays to create a 3D computer model of the ear. The model guided the bioprinter, which was loaded with biodegradable polymer materials, to form a scaffold in the shape of the ear. The scientists seeded the scaffold with cartilage cells (these cells form the firm, elastic type of connective tissue found in various parts of the body, including the outer ear) and skin cells. Atala incorporated tiny

FERTILE GROUND: 3D-PRINTED OVARIES

Cancer treatments such as chemotherapy and radiation that target the abdomen can sometimes damage the ovaries of girls and women, leaving them infertile or with unhealthy hormone imbalances. If this happens to young cancer survivors, they may need supplemental hormones to trigger puberty. That's what prompted scientists in the school of medicine and engineering at Northwestern University in Chicago, Illinois, to collaborate in making 3D-printed ovaries. These ovaries could restore fertility and hormonal health to girls and women who needed them.

In 2017 the Northwestern team created artificial ovaries for infertile mice. A 3D printer used gelatin, or a hydrogel made from broken-down collagen, as the ink to lay down a scaffold structure. The finished product looked a bit like something you might build with Lincoln Logs, but each scaffold measured 0.6 by 0.6 inches (15 by 15 mm). The team carefully placed mouse follicles—round biological structures with an immature egg cell surrounded by hormone-producing cells—into the scaffolds. The scaffold allowed room for the egg cells to mature, grow, and release from the follicles. It also had space for blood vessels to distribute hormones throughout the bloodstream.

The research team then implanted the 3D-printed ovaries into female mice whose ovaries the team had removed. Each mouse's own blood supply soon hooked up to the implants, providing the cells with the nutrients and oxygen they needed to survive. Of the seven mice that mated after receiving artificial ovaries, three gave birth. The mother mice produced milk for the pups, which later grew up to have pups of their own. So the mouse life cycle appeared to carry on with no harm to the mother mouse or to her pups and their pups.

In the future, the Northwestern team is hoping that girls and women can have their follicles harvested and saved before undergoing cancer treatment. After their treatment is finished, surgeons can then implant the follicles in an artificial ovary. The women and girls also would have the option to use donated follicles if their own are damaged.

blood vessel-like channels into the design of the ear to allow necessary nutrients and oxygen to be transported to the cells. After about six months, the hydrogel had biodegraded, while the seeded cartilage and skin cells grew and multiplied to form an ear composed entirely of human cells. The team implanted a number of ears under the skin of mice—and they thrived, with the mice's blood vessels growing into the channels Atala created. (Yes, a mouse with a human ear on its side looks strange.)

ENGINEERING BETTER KNEES

"Everybody seems to have some story about their knees," said Gilda Barabino, dean of engineering and professor of biomedical engineering at City College, New York. "If not their own, somebody else's!"

Often those knee stories revolve around damage to the cartilage, which covers the surface of joints. It acts as a shock absorber and allows the bones to slide over one another. It can become damaged through sudden injury—often sports-related—or through gradual wear and tear. Minor cartilage injuries may get better within a few weeks, but more severe damage may eventually require surgery, which is not always successful.

Cartilage would seem to be a simple tissue to engineer. It is made of just one cell type—the chondrocyte. This cell type has no blood vessels or nerves. But you can't just put chondrocytes on a scaffold and culture them with nutrients and growth factors, or proteins that help cells divide and multiply, and expect to get good cartilage tissue. The result would be too mechanically weak for a tissue that has to bear a lot of weight and be elastic.

The cells need a mechanical stimulation to encourage them to produce extracellular matrix (ECM), a biological glue that hold the cells of a tissue together. In the case of cartilage, extracellular matrix is made of collagen and other molecules. So lab technicians culture chondrocytes on biodegradable scaffolds in bioreactors, or cylindrical vessels that stir things up. That mechanical stress encourages chondrocytes to produce more of this biological glue. Barabino applied her engineering expertise

ENGINEERING CARTILAGE TISSUE

This infographic from Gilda Barabino shows the key elements in cartilage tissue engineering. The bioreactor (A) is a controllable environment in which to grow tissue replacements. The reactor also provides mechanical stimuli to encourage tissues to develop. Tiny synthetic biological carriers (C) deliver nutrients, proteins, and essential biomolecules such as growth factors (E) to cultured cells (D) on

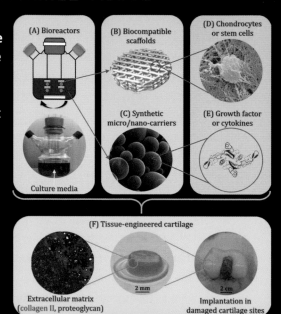

(A) Bioreactors

(B) Biocompatible scaffolds

(D) Chondrocytes or stem cells

(C) Synthetic micro/nano-carriers

(E) Growth factor or cytokines

Culture media

(F) Tissue-engineered cartilage

Extracellular matrix (collagen II, proteoglycan)

2 mm

Implantation in damaged cartilage sites

2 cm

a scaffold (B). When these elements are combined appropriately, the bioreactor creates functional tissue-engineered cartilage (F). The cartilage can then be implanted into host cartilage to regenerate the tissue.

in fluid mechanics to develop a more efficient bioreactor. She calls it her "crazy little wavy wall reactor," and it stirs the cells even faster to make even more ECM without damaging them.

Barabino's cartilage has yet to be tested in clinical trials. "A lot of the research we do in my lab is basic; we're still trying to get a fundamental understanding of the relationships between the environments in which we are cultivating the tissues and the properties you end up with," Barabino said. "But ultimately, you want to . . . commercialize the approach. Because if there's not a need for this work, what are we doing in the lab?"

FIXING A LUNG

Nearly twenty-five million people in the United States suffer from end-stage lung disease. Lung transplants are the only good option for many of these patients, but the demand for lungs greatly outweighs the supply. Researchers and doctors want to find a way to build new lungs. But it's not that easy.

"The lung is unbelievably complex," said Gordana Vunjak-Novakovic, professor of biomedical engineering and biomedical sciences at Columbia University in New York City. Forty to forty-five different cell types make up the airways, she explained, the tubular branches, or bronchi, that divide into ever-smaller branches. Blood vessels entwine throughout the airways, creating a surface for air exchange that is the size of a tennis court. "To think about making a piece of lung from scratch, like we would make bone or muscle—it's impossible," she said.

Transplant surgeons told Vunjak-Novakovic that if she could find a way to fix just part of a lung, it would go a long way toward addressing the donor shortage issue. "Four out of five donated lungs are rejected by the transplant teams," Vunjak-Novakovic said. The donated lungs are often from people who suffered terrible injuries before dying. Acids from the stomach may have gotten into the lungs, or the lung tissues may have suffered from a lack of oxygen. They wouldn't be able to deliver enough oxygen to the recipient.

The surgeons told Vunjak-Novakovic that most donated lungs need to be improved by only 10 to 20 percent to be workable. So Vunjak-Novakovic developed a method to improve the quality of donated lungs. She removes the cells from the damaged parts of the donor lungs, preserving the extracellular matrix that holds everything together. Then she seeds the matrix with iPS from the recipient—all the while keeping the lung healthy with a system that provides it with blood flow and oxygen.

"If you think about it, even if we cannot salvage all four [out of five donor lungs], even if we salvage two, we increase the number of

SOLUTIONS TO THE ORGAN SHORTAGE CRISIS

The Organ Procurement and Transplantation Network is a Virginia-based organization that connects patients to donated organs. The network also collects and analyzes data, reporting that as of March 2018, nearly 115,000 Americans were on the waiting list for a lifesaving transplant. Yet only 5,448 of those people received transplants because fewer than 3,000 organ donors were available. So a huge gap separates organ supply from organ demand.

About 50 percent of transplanted organs will fail within five to ten years, usually because the recipient's immune system rejects the donor tissue. The immune system protects us from microbes (bacteria), viruses, and other harmful things. Microbes and viruses, as well as human cells, carry proteins called antigens on their surfaces. Foreign antigens entering the body are a red flag to the immune system, which acts swiftly to attack the invading cells.

However, the immune system doesn't distinguish between a disease-causing microbe and a lifesaving organ. If the antigens are foreign, the immune system attacks. No two people, except identical twins, have identical tissue antigens. Doctors who work with transplant patients try to find the closest match possible between donor and recipient. The more similar the antigens between the two people, the less likely the organ will be rejected. Even so, people with organ transplants usually have to take drugs to suppress the immune system so it will not attack the new organ. Suppressing the immune system also makes the person more vulnerable to infections. It's a serious trade-off.

So tissue-engineered organs are the dream of transplant surgeons. They would relieve the donor organ shortage by providing more organs that are healthy. And immune rejection would not be a problem because the organs would be made from the patient's own cells.

acceptable lungs by three times. It's huge; the patients don't have to wait forever to get lungs," said Vunjak-Novakovic.

Like Barabino, Vunjak-Novakovic is also investigating ways of making better cartilage in the lab. Vunjak-Novakovic used human stem cells derived from fat tissue to make functional cartilage. She is also working to repair large bone defects and injuries in the head and face to create bone grafts using lab-grown living bone. She and her research team take the joints of calves, carve the bones into the desired shape, and strip them of all their living cells to create a scaffold for the new bone graft. They seed the scaffolding with multipotent stem cells taken from human fat tissue and feed them with the right combination of nutrients, growth factors, and oxygen to instruct the cells to transform into bone cells, or osteoblasts. Once the bone graft fully forms, doctors can implant it onto the defective bone, where it naturally integrates with the existing bone. By using the patient's own stem cells to create the bone graft, they hope to avoid the problem of immune rejection. Vunjak-Novakovic and her colleagues have formed a start-up company, EpiBone, to market their technology.

ORGAN-ON-A-CHIP

In a 2016 TEDx Talk, Kacey Ronaldson tells the story of her Uncle Billy. As a youth basketball referee, he was sidelined when he was diagnosed with cancer. Uncle Billy joined a clinical trial designed to test a promising new drug treatment that he and his doctors hoped would cure his disease. At first, it seemed to work, but soon he was back in the hospital. He entered one clinical trial after another, with similar outcomes.

His story is all too common—a drug that successfully targets one person's cancer cells might not be effective against another person's cancer cells. Each person's unique genetic makeup determines how that individual will respond to many drugs. Age, gender, ethnicity, and preexisting conditions—all play a role. The best-selling drug for depression helps just one out of nine people. One out of twenty people with asthma responds to the best-selling treatment for that condition.

THE TRADITIONAL DRUG
DEVELOPMENT PROCESS

Discovering, developing, and getting FDA approval for new drugs to treat diseases is a long and expensive process. It begins with basic research aimed at understanding the disease itself. Researchers identify a target—the gene or protein involved in the disease. This basic research often uses animals such as mice or rats. The aim is to discover whether modifying that target might improve human health and how. This research can last from months to decades. Armed with that knowledge, researchers can proceed to the first step in drug development.

Step 1. Discovery and development. Researchers test tens of thousands of chemicals from a library of potential drugs to determine which bind to and affect the function of the target. They may refine the chemical makeup of potential drugs to improve how well they interact with the target and make sure that the drug affects only the target rather than other cells or molecules in the body. This step helps prevent unwanted side effects. It can take as long as two and a half years, at a cost of more than $6 billion. This step eliminates many of the potential drugs, like players voted off the island in the TV show *Survivor*. Each subsequent step in drug development votes more drugs off the research island.

Step 2. Preclinical research. Once researchers have narrowed their list of drug candidates down to a few hundred compounds, they begin to test them for safety and effectiveness, both in vivo and in animals, often rats and mice. These studies provide detailed information on dosing and toxicity levels. Usually only a handful of drugs make the cut. This process can take about four years to complete, costing more than $6 billion. Next, the researchers must apply to the FDA for approval to test the drugs in humans.

Step 3. Clinical trials. When the FDA has determined that a potential drug is safe to study in humans, the researchers can begin a series of clinical trials, or studies. Phase 1 studies typically include twenty to one hundred healthy volunteers or people with the target disease. The purpose of the study is to determine the safety and dosage of the drug, and it can last several months. About 70 percent of drugs tested in phase 1 studies move on to the next phase. Up to several hundred people with the targeted disease participate in the phase 2 study, which can last several months to two years. The purpose of the phase 2 study is to determine the drug's effectiveness and side effects. Only 33 percent of drugs move on to the next phase. Researchers recruit three hundred to three thousand volunteers with the disease for the phase 3 study, lasting one to four years. Researchers pay close attention to how well the drug works, and monitor the volunteers closely for any harmful side effects. About 25 to 30 percent of the drugs from this phase move on to long-term studies with a larger group of volunteers.

Step 4. FDA drug review. Once researchers are satisfied that their new drug works and is safe to use in humans, they submit all of their data in a New Drug Application to the FDA for approval to market the drug. FDA approval can take six to ten months. Even after the drug is approved and on the market, the FDA continues to monitor the safety of the drug for months and even years.

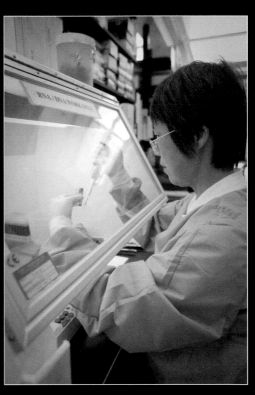

A scientist at the National Institute of Allergy and Infectious Diseases works with genetic material as part of her vaccine research.

Ronaldson notes that eight out of ten drugs tested in clinical trials fail to get approval. Why? The drugs are first tested on rodents—often mice. A drug that cures cancer in a mouse may not work in humans because we are not rodents. "It takes years and years and billions of dollars just to get a drug to market," Ronaldson said. So no pharmaceutical company would ever use traditional methods to develop a drug specifically tailored to help just one person such as Uncle Billy.

Ronaldson is a postdoctoral fellow in Vunjak-Novakovic's lab at Columbia University. With her and others, Ronaldson cofounded a start-up company called Tara. (Tara is the name of a beautiful mountain in Serbia, Vunjak-Novakovic's native country.) She and her colleagues are among the growing number of scientists creating tiny "organs-on-a-chip." These miniature biological versions of human hearts, livers, ovaries, and other body parts can test the effects of new drugs on human organs and tissues. They may well be the best way to speed up the pace of new drug development and make it easier for doctors to determine the best treatment for individual patients.

Ronaldson, who specializes in engineering cardiac, or heart, tissue, explained the process. The first step is to create induced pluripotent stem cells from a donor. By using the right combination of nutrients and growth factors, she coaxes these iPS cells into becoming cardiac cells, which begin to beat in a petri dish just like any other heart cells. The goal is to make those cells act like mini hearts and not just independent beating cells, so Ronaldson has found a way of engineering a cell environment that mimics our body's environment. She puts 1.5 million cells into a vessel with two tiny, flexible polymer pillars. The heart cells begin to grow and divide, attaching themselves to the pillars. Two anchors on each end of the pillars give the cells something to beat against. Ronaldson stimulates the cells with electrical pulses to help them mature—that may take up to twelve weeks. "We want them to beat with a strong force," she said. Because pluripotent stem cells are like fetal cells (the fetal stage follows the embryonic stage about eight weeks after fertilization), the very young cardiac cells resemble a fetal heart. "Your heart continues to go through a lot of development until you're about three years old, and so we want our heart model to be as mature as it can be," she said. The cardiac cells pump away, just like the heart in a human chest. Ronaldson can measure the effects of certain drugs on the mini hearts. Do they make them beat faster or slower? Do the drugs cause the cells to beat irregularly, which can be a fatal response to certain drugs?

Human body organs don't exist on separate chips. They communicate with one another through hormones and other signals. And drugs designed to treat one organ—the heart, for example—can often have damaging side effects on another organ, such as the liver. So Vunjak-Novakovic and her colleagues are creating multiple organs-on-a-chip—something more like a body-on-a-chip. Think about driving through the suburbs, Ronaldson said. "All of the houses look alike from the outside; all of the building materials are the same. But for developing miniature organs we can customize the interior of each [one] to support whatever tissue we want to put inside." Like houses in the suburbs, culture chambers where cells grow can be connected by "streets"—channels similar to blood vessels through which a blood substitute can flow. When a new drug enters the chambers, researchers can see how it impacts the various tissues inside.

Ultimately, organs-on-a-chip will test potential drug treatments for individual patients, like Uncle Billy, which may take three to six months. In the future, that may be quicker, Ronaldson said. Uncle Billy died soon after Ronaldson gave her TEDx Talk, but she hopes that her research will help others in need of just the right drug for them.

BRAINPOWER

I n the movie *Mad Max: Fury Road,* Imperator Furiosa (played by Charlize Theron) is an amputee who wears a prosthetic arm apparently powered by her brain. The movie is science fiction, but the ability to control external devices—such as prostheses or robots—just by thinking about them has become a reality. It's made possible by a technology called the brain-computer interface, which picks up electrical signals from the brain, analyzes them, and transmits them to machines or even to other people.

The brain is made of about one hundred billion neurons, or nerve cells. The brain, along with the spinal cord, is the control center of the entire nervous system. Every thought, emotion, movement, or sensation is coordinated through neuronal communication. So, for example, if someone thinks, "Hey, I'm thirsty; I need a drink of water," neurons in the brain send out instructions in the form of electrical

A real-world technology known as the brain-computer interface plays a role in the 2015 postapocalyptic action movie *Mad Max: Fury Road*. The character Imperator Furiosa (*left*) uses BCI to control her prosthetic arm.

signals to the neurons in the peripheral nervous system—the nervous system outside of the brain and spinal cord. Those signals stimulate muscles that allow the person to pick up a glass of water, lift it to the mouth, open the mouth, drink, and swallow. We don't actually have to think about this; it's an automatic process.

The story of brain-computer interfaces (BCIs) goes back to 1924. That year German scientist Hans Berger attached electrodes, or conductors used to establish an electrical current, to the scalp of a volunteer and recorded the signals that person's neurons emitted. Berger's technology, the electroencephalograph (EEG), detects brain waves. It's an invaluable diagnostic tool to identify the abnormal brain waves in conditions such as epilepsy, sleep disorders, and head injuries. The EEG also has allowed scientists to map the regions of the

BERGER, TELEPATHY, AND THE EEG

Hans Berger's invention of the electroencephalograph was inspired by a bizarre event that happened in 1892 when he was nineteen years old and was serving a year in the German military. One spring morning, he was riding a horse that was pulling heavy artillery for a military training exercise. Suddenly, the horse reared. Berger was thrown from the horse, landing just in front of the wheel of an artillery gun. The horse stopped just in time, sparing a terrified Berger from certain death.

That evening Berger received a telegram from his father, asking about his son's well-being. Berger later learned that his older sister had had a terrible feeling that something awful had happened to Berger that morning. She had urged her father to contact him. Berger, who had never before received a telegram from his family, was struck by the coincidence. He became convinced that his intense feelings of terror had somehow become matter and reached his sister hundreds of miles away. He believed they had communicated through telepathy.

Hans Berger was a German psychiatrist known for developing the EEG. He is pictured here in 1930.

After completing his military service, Berger began studying medicine, determined to understand the relationship between mind and matter. By then neurologists understood that the human brain sends electrical waves. Berger was convinced that these waves held the answers to his questions about the mind-matter connection. Most of his scientific peers dismissed his research. But it led to the development of the EEG.

We'll never know what was behind the ominous feeling Berger's sister had, and he never got to the bottom of it either. However, we know that scientists demonstrated human brain-to-brain communication using brain-computer interfaces in 2013—and that it involves electroencephalographs.

brain responsible for different tasks. Raising a hand causes a flurry of electrical activity in one part of the brain. A flash of light evokes a response in another part of the brain.

In the 1960s, researchers began to wonder: what if they could send signals, not to the peripheral nervous system but to a computer? In 1964 Dr. Grey Walter at the Burden Neurological Institute in Bristol, England, did just that. He implanted electrodes directly into the motor areas of a patient's brain. (The patient was undergoing brain surgery for other reasons and had agreed to the experiment.) When the patient recovered from surgery, Walter asked him to press a button to advance a slide projector. The resulting brain activity was sent to a computer. Next, Walter connected the computer to that same slide projector and sure enough, it advanced even if the man simply thought about pressing the button!

The potential applications for brain-computer interfaces are amazing, particularly for people with brain stem or spinal cord injuries, or for amputees (like the fictional Furiosa!). In clinical trials, patients with severe muscle weakness or paralysis who are hooked up to a BCI system can move a cursor around a computer screen to spell out words—just by thinking about it. Patients with limited physical mobility could also potentially use a BCI to control wheelchairs or a robot assistant.

"Anytime anybody has a spinal cord injury, they typically lose the ability to move," said Abidemi Bolu Ajiboye, assistant professor of biomedical engineering at Case Western Reserve University in Cleveland, Ohio. Ajiboye's team is part of a larger collaboration of hospitals and universities called BrainGate. The collaboration focuses on developing BCI technologies. "The signals in the brain cannot get past the spinal cord into . . . the peripheral nerves and muscles in the limbs," he said. In 2014 Ajiboye led a team of scientists and physicians who restored arm and hand movements to Bill Kochevar, a man with quadriplegia (the paralysis of all four limbs). The fifty-six-year-old was paralyzed from his shoulders down following a bicycle accident eight years earlier.

Technicians can record brain signals in a couple of different ways. With

EEGs they usually attach electrodes to the outer scalp in a fairly simple and painless procedure. But those signals are not of the highest resolution, Ajiboye said. "Suppose you are at a concert, and listening to an orchestra," Ajiboye said. "If you are onstage, your ear will be able to discern the different instruments quite clearly: the violin, and the cello, from the rest of the orchestra. If you're across the street, you won't be able to discern the individual instruments as well; you'll just hear the general music. In the same way, when [the electrodes] are outside of the brain—that is, across the street—we can only record the general activity of the brain." To get a clear picture of what the brain patterns mean relative to the desired movement, the electrodes need to be inside the brain, onstage.

Ajiboye's team implanted two sets of tiny electrodes, each set about the size of a baby aspirin, on the surface of Kochevar's motor cortex, the part of the brain responsible for movement. With this BCI, he learned how to control a virtual reality arm on a computer screen. The arrays recorded the brain signals created whenever Kochevar imagined moving the arm and passed that information to the computer. It took him just a few minutes to get the hang of it. After four months of training, the researchers thought he was ready to control his own arm and hand.

Next, the team implanted thirty-six additional electrodes in Kochevar's right arm. These electrodes were placed near the muscles controlling his hand, wrist, arm, elbow, and shoulder. When Kochevar thought about moving his own arm, the BCI relayed his brain signals to the electrodes in his arm, which sent out electrical pulses that stimulated his muscles.

Kochevar was the first recipient of an implanted BCI and muscle-stimulating system. In a video interview, he said, "It was amazing, because I thought about moving my arm and it did. I ate a pretzel, I drank water . . . one day, we had some mashed potatoes, and lo and behold, I was able to eat the mashed potatoes really well." People with quadriplegia often say that the things they miss most are the ability to scratch an itch, feed themselves, or perform other simple functions on their own. Kochevar could do all of that.

Biomedical engineering professor Abidemi Bolu Ajiboye specializes in BCI technology at Case Western Reserve University in Ohio. Here he fits a volunteer with electrodes and virtual reality 3D glasses to teach him how to work with a virtual hand on a computer screen. Eventually, this technology will enable people with paralysis to manipulate prosthetic devices using just their brain signals.

Kochevar's experience with the BCI was limited to his work with researchers in the laboratory. The technology has a long way to go before it can be useful for the many thousands of people who could benefit from it in their everyday lives. The main hurdles—or challenges, as Ajiboye calls them—involve finance, engineering, and science. The technology devices won't be cheap, and insurance companies must be convinced they are worth covering. Kochevar's implants were connected to two large cylinders that sit atop his head. From there, a cable connected them to a rack of computers. "We'd like to be able to miniaturize that rack of computers to the size of a cell phone so that it would be completely portable," Ajiboye said, "and to make the system completely wireless and invisible to the outside world."

And then there's the problem of sensory feedback—or rather, a lack of it. It's hard for people like Kochevar as well as those who wear prosthetics to carry out tasks such as picking up objects without crushing them or losing their grip, because they can't feel what they are doing. Many amputees who use prosthetics don't like to shake hands or hold the hand of a loved one because they fear hurting them. Dustin Tyler, one of Ajiboye's colleagues at Case Western, has designed a new system that uses pressure sensors on a prosthetic hand. The pressure sensors send signals to a portable device that sends electrical pulses to nerve bundles in the arm. The nerves then pass those signals to the brain. One man testing the system, Keith Vonderheuvel, describes picking up his granddaughter with both hands: "I could actually feel that I was holding her and not squeezing too tight, and she gave me a big hug. That one just—that gets to me."

The technology could have much broader applications, according to Tyler. Feeling is an important sense for analyzing and understanding the physical and emotional environments in which we live. So BCI's could one day assist the operator of a robotic explorer on the ocean floor or a bomb squad robot in their work.

ANIMAL CUES

Another challenge is that conventional electrodes are usually made of wire or some other stiff material. Over time electrodes implanted into the brain can cause damage and scar brain tissue. The brain is soft and squishy, not unlike Jell-O. "If you put a nail into Jell-O, and you shake the Jell-O, you would damage the Jell-O," explained Jeffrey Capadona, associate professor of biomedical engineering at Case Western Reserve University. "That's basically what's happening in the brain. If you stick small needles into the surface of the brain, and they're not moving because they're attached to the skull, but the brain is moving, the injuries are never ending."

Ideally, researchers would like to have electrodes made of a soft material that won't damage brain tissue. Placing a soft electrode into the soft brain tissue is difficult—like trying to stick a wet noodle into the Jell-O-like material of the brain. "But if you start with an uncooked piece of spaghetti and slip it into the brain, it softens so that it's like a wet noodle and doesn't cause more damage," Capadona said. Pasta is not a good material for electrodes, because it breaks down and it doesn't conduct electricity. Instead, Capadona looked to nature for inspiration. He found it in the sea cucumber. The animals can quickly change the stiffness of their skin in response to environmental cues, simply by crossing or uncrossing collagen fibers. Capadona's lab created polymer fibers that could do the same thing.

As with most electronic devices, brain implants are becoming smaller. While that's good for minimizing damage, those tiny things are hard to place inside the brain. Capadona found the answer in nature: the pesky mosquito. The mosquito's mouth has six thin, needlelike parts. Two of them have tiny teeth that let the mosquito saw through skin. Another set of parts holds the skin tissues apart, while another strawlike needle part pierces a blood vessel so that the mosquito can drink her fill. (Female mosquitoes are the ones that bite humans.) Capadona's lab is testing a 3D-printed device inspired by the mosquito's mouthparts to see if the device can implant the tiny devices in animal brains without causing damage.

Ajiboye estimates that some of the scientific and engineering hurdles of BCI technology can be overcome in the next ten to fifteen years. But that doesn't mean the BCI system that uses implanted electrodes will be available that soon. Other factors, he says, have to fall into place first, including approval from the FDA.

CYBORG FUTURE

Much of the current BCI research is geared toward helping people with disabilities. BCI may be useful in many other environments. External EEG devices work well for some applications, especially as researchers figure out better ways to filter out noise and improve the algorithms, or equations, that support the software. For example, you can pretend you have telekinetic, or mind control, powers with a brain-controlled helicopter made by a company called Neurosky. Another company, Neurable, is working on a sci-fi virtual reality game in which the gamer wears an electroencephalograph headband that connects to a virtual reality headset.

The future of BCI is more than just fun and games. Facebook is exploring ways of building a BCI that will allow users to type with the mind without

THE ETHICS OF BRAIN COMPUTER INTERFACES

In the 1995 film *Batman Forever*, the Riddler creates a box that transmits brain waves through a TV to create 3D images. "Soon my little 'Box' will be on countless TVs around the world, feeding me credit card numbers, bank codes, sexual fantasies, and little white lies. Into my head they'll go. Victory is inevitable."

That movie reference seemed eerily prophetic when Nielsen, the company that tracks what people watch, listen to, and buy, acquired NeuroFocus in 2011. NeuroFocus uses brain waves and other physical data, including eye tracking, heart rate, and facial coding, to gauge the attitudes and behaviors of consumers who participate in Nielsen surveys and who agree to allow the company to monitor their reactions. This includes behaviors that the individuals themselves may not be consciously aware of.

The potential for the invasion of privacy is just one area of concern for neuroethicists. These experts study the ethical issues arising from new neuroengineering technologies. Is it right to access and potentially use an individual's unconscious thoughts? Is privacy as important as technological advance? If so, how do we protect privacy?

Neuroethicists also think about accountability. It's easy to imagine a scenario in which a person thinks something like, "I want to punch

the need for invasive implants. The plan is to use optical imaging to scan a person's brain one hundred times a second as that person speaks to themselves and then translate the speech into text. The goal is to allow people to type one hundred words a minute, far faster than we can type on a phone. In 2015 Facebook chief executive officer Mark Zuckerberg predicted that people will one day use BCI to go beyond sharing cat videos and prom photos to sharing "full sensory and emotional experiences" online.

Michio Kaku, a physicist at City College, New York, told NBC News that "the internet will eventually be replaced by a brain-net, in which we can experience emotions, memories and sensations. Of course, teenagers are going to go crazy on Facebook—they'll share the memory of their first kiss, their first date, the senior prom. All those emotions and hormones pumping away, on Facebook!"

him out"—that the person would never actually carry out. But what if the computer in a BCI is unable to assess the ethics in a thought? What if it carries out the punch or leads the human in the BCI to carry it out? Who is responsible if that were to happen? And could brain-to-brain interfaces be used to control or coerce the behavior of another person?

Elon Musk envisions a day when biological intelligence will merge with machine intelligence. This type of neuroenhancement technology will be costly at first. Will it be available only to those who can afford it? Will the rich control people who can't afford the technology? What are the limits?

Neuroethicists also think about the issue of personhood. How do we define what it means to be an individual human being when our brains are in a symbiotic relationship with a computer? What about when the brains of two individuals are wired together?

Many researchers and ethicists see great potential in BCI devices. At the same time, they are aware that BCI, like many advances in science and engineering, holds real challenges for society. The discovery of petroleum as a cheap and plentiful source of fuel in the nineteenth century revolutionized the way we lived, worked, and traveled—and led us to our current climate crisis. We—scientists, ethicists, and the public—must think about the potential harm as well as the benefits of new technologies.

Elon Musk, chief executive officer of Tesla, which makes Tesla electric self-driving cars and the SpaceX spaceship, wants to take BCI a step—or perhaps a giant leap—further. In 2016 he started the company Neuralink to develop an even more advanced brain-computer interface. At the World Government Summit in Dubai, United Arab Emirates, in February 2017, he said that increasingly sophisticated artificial intelligence systems and robots will lead to mass unemployment. With more robots, fewer human workers will be necessary. His solution? Merge biological intelligence such as BCI with machine artificial intelligence. If we fail to do so, he said, we would risk becoming "house cats"—an amusing pet—to artificial intelligence. "I don't love the idea of being a house cat," he told the summit. His idea is to create an injectable neural lace—a mesh that fits on the human brain to allow it to "achieve

Futuristic television and film often portray technologies that are far ahead of their time. Will human-to-human brain interface be a reality one day, as it has been since the 1960s in the Star Trek universe? (This still is from the 2013 film *Star Trek Into Darkness*. Zachary Quinto, *left*, played Mr. Spock. Chris Pine, *right*, played Captain James T. Kirk.)

symbiosis [a mutually beneficial relationship between two things] with machines."

Musk envisions a two-way BCI. It will transmit signals to the brain and from there to a paralyzed limb or a machine. It also will seamlessly download signals from a computer directly to the brain, allowing it to access the computing power of the internet. Plugging humans into the internet, he argues, could make us smarter, help with decision-making, and even improve our memory. Critics, however, worry about the ethical implications of plugging the human brain directly into cyberspace.

A VULCAN MIND MELD FOR EARTHLINGS

In the Star Trek universe, Mr. Spock and other Vulcans were able to form a telepathic link, or "mind meld," between two individuals. The initiator would simply touch fingertips to the recipient's temples. The physical contact allowed the two to share memories, thoughts, and sensory impressions.

In our earthling universe, researchers at the University of Washington in Seattle have performed a human-to-human brain interface. In this scenario, one researcher sends a brain signal through the internet to control the hand movements of another researcher across campus. It's a kind of earthling mind meld, perhaps more akin to telepathy.

In 2013 Rajesh Rao, a professor of computer science and engineering at the University of Washington, sat in his lab wearing an electrode-studded EEG cap hooked up to an EEG machine. His colleague, Andrea Stocco, an assistant professor in psychology, sat in his lab a mile (1.6 km) across campus. He was wearing a purple swimming cap with a magnetic coil directly over his left motor cortex, the part of the brain that controls hand movement. He was wearing noise-canceling earbuds so he would not be distracted by any outside noises.

Rao played a simple video game on a computer screen. When he wanted to fire a cannon at a target, he imagined moving his right hand onto the cursor (careful not to actually move his hand), causing the cursor to hit the Fire target at the top of the computer screen. A computer sent Rao's Fire brain signal to a computer in Stocco's lab, which activated the magnetic coil on Stocco's head. Stocco was not looking at a computer screen, yet almost immediately, his right index finger moved to push the Space bar on a keyboard in front of him, as if firing the cannon. This was the exact movement Rao imagined making. Rao's brain signal had directed Stocco to move his finger.

The Vulcan mind meld is used in the *Star Trek* series mostly between two Vulcans. But it is sometimes used between a Vulcan and another life-form. The earthling mind meld doesn't have to be a strictly human thing either. Scientists at Harvard have created a brain-to-brain interface between a human and a rat, with the human causing the rat's tail to move. At the Korea Advanced Institute of Science and Technology in Daejeon, South Korea, scientists have developed a system where human thoughts can control the movement of turtles.

So it's not exactly a Vulcan mind meld yet.

EDITING THE HUMAN GENOME

D anish botanist Wilhelm Johannsen coined the word *gene* in 1909 to describe the fundamental units of heredity. Long before that, people were tinkering with the genomes (the complete set of genetic material in an organism) of plants and animals. Selective breeding, or artificial selection, gave us Great Danes and Chihuahuas, and it transformed a wild grass known as teosinte into plump ears of corn. But selective breeding is slow and the outcomes are not always predictable.

In the 1970s, the gene tinkerers really got going. Scientists developed recombinant DNA technology. It allows researchers to cut genetic instructions from the DNA of one species and paste them into another to produce desired traits. For example, scientists have introduced an antifreeze gene from Arctic flounder into strawberries to extend their growing season in northern climates. Using recombinant DNA techniques,

TRADITIONAL RECOMBINANT DNA TECHNOLOGY

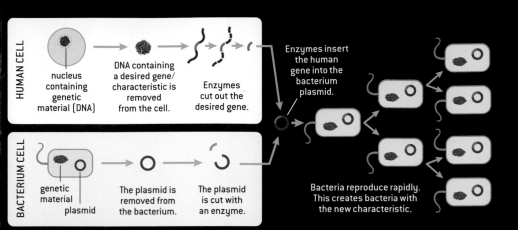

In traditional recombinant DNA technology, researchers can take genetic information from the DNA of one species and insert it into another species to create a third variant with a desired trait. This infographic shows the technology with human and bacterial cells.

scientists have created bacteria that can make human insulin and many other medically useful substances. Genetic engineering has transformed medicine, agriculture, industrial chemical production, and basic research itself.

By the 1980s and 1990s, scientists were beginning to use recombinant DNA techniques to treat humans in clinical trials. In one trial, scientists were able to treat children with severe combined immune deficiency caused by a missing gene coding for an important enzyme, adenosine deaminase. They used a virus to introduce a healthy adenosine deaminase gene into the T cells (a type of immune cell) of these patients. A significant number of the children got better.

But these conventional gene therapy techniques were initially very time-consuming. And the technology wasn't always precise, sometimes inserting genes into a random place in the genome. Random placement can lead to mutations, which can trigger the formation of a cancer gene.

CRISPR TECHNOLOGY

1.

defective DNA strand

Scientists identify a defective DNA strand to be cut out and modified.

2.

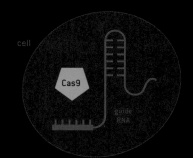

cell

Cas9

guide RNA

They create guide RNA that has the same genomic code as the defective DNA. This is combined in a cell with an enzyme called Cas9, which acts like scissors to cut the defective DNA.

3.

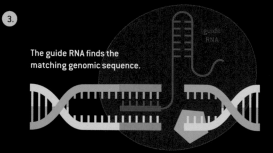

guide RNA

The guide RNA finds the matching genomic sequence.

Then the Cas9 cuts the strand making a break in the DNA helix.

4.

healthy DNA strand

Cells are able to detect and repair broken DNA. A healthy strand of DNA is inserted at the cut site and enzymes repair it.

In 1999 an eighteen-year-old boy died after receiving gene therapy.

But by the early twenty-first century, genetic engineers had added some new techniques to their DNA toolbox, notably CRISPR-Cas9. This technique allows them to edit the DNA of nearly any living organism relatively cheaply, with more precision and speed than ever before.

WHAT IS CRISPR-CAS9?

CRISPR-Cas9, or just CRISPR, pronounced like the word *crisper*, stands for the unwieldy phrase Clustered Regularly Interspaced Short Palindromic Repeats. It refers to specialized stretches of DNA in bacteria. Cas9 is a scissorlike protein

The CRISPR-Cas9 technology, uses a naturally occurring gene-editing system in bacteria. It's exciting because it is faster, cheaper, more accurate, and more efficient than traditional recombinant DNA technology.

that can cut strands of DNA. The CRISPR sequences, along with the Cas9 protein, are part of the immune system of bacteria.

Bacteria, like just about every other living thing, are under constant assault from viruses. If the bacteria manage to kill off invading viruses, they use enzymes, or protein molecules, that set off specific biochemical reactions, to chop up the remains of the virus's genetic code. The bacteria store the remains in CRISPR sequences. When viruses attack again, the bacteria produce special enzymes, called Cas9. They carry around those stored bits of genetic code as RNA, or ribonucleic acid, the molecule that copies portions of genetic code and transports those copies to the cellular factories that make proteins. Each gene contained in a DNA molecule has a unique, complementary RNA molecule. Much as a police officer might use a mug shot to identify a criminal, Cas9 compares its CRISPR sequences to the invading virus's RNA. If they match, the Cas9 enzyme slices into the virus's DNA to chop it up and get rid of it. It's a clever and precise molecular scalpel.

Scientists trying to understand how the CRISPR-Cas9 system works discovered that they could feed artificial RNA—a lab-made CRISPR sequence coded to match a specific DNA sequence—to the Cas9 enzyme. The engineered enzyme would then search for any genome with the matching DNA code, not just viruses, and start slicing. Researchers soon realized that they could use the CRISPR technique to silence and even repair specific genes.

Matthew Porteus, an associate professor at Stanford University in California and a scientific cofounder and advisory board member of CRISPR Therapeutics, has proposed a clinical trial to use CRISPR-Cas9 technology to repair the stem cells of people with sickle cell disease. Sickle-cell disease is a serious blood disorder caused by a single defective gene that makes hemoglobin, the protein in red blood cells that delivers oxygen from the lungs to the rest of the body. Their strategy begins with creating a CRISPR sequence that matches the defective sequence of the gene and feeding it to the Cas9 enzyme. Doctors would then take blood stem cells from the patient, add that CRISPR-Cas9 enzyme, and let the

CAN THE WOOLLY MAMMOTH MAKE A COMEBACK?

George Church, a geneticist at Harvard, is one of the pioneers of CRISPR and synthetic biology. He is legendary for his willingness to take on big engineering and scientific challenges.

One of Church's start-up companies is using gene editing to try to reverse the effects of aging in dogs and eventually in humans. He is also using CRISPR to alter sixty-two pig genes with the goal of safely transplanting pig organs into humans. This could help solve the organ donor crisis.

He may be best known for his interest in bringing back the long-extinct woolly mammoth—or something like it. Using samples of mammoth tissue, naturally preserved in permafrost—a thick layer of permanently frozen soil under the surface, mostly in polar regions—scientists have sequenced the entire woolly mammoth genome. Church's aim is to introduce the mammoth genes that code for thick layers of fat, long shaggy hair, and blood suited for cold weather into the genome of the closely related—and living—Asian elephant. Church's team has made forty-five mammoth gene edits to the Asian elephant's genome.

The team will eventually have made enough gene edits to create an elephant embryo with all the mammoth traits that allow it to survive in the cold. However, Asian elephants are an endangered species. Most people, including Church, agree that implanting an engineered embryo into the womb of an Asian elephant is not an ethical move. So Church hopes to one day develop artificial wombs in the lab.

Church's motivation for bringing back the woolly mammoth goes beyond a gee-whiz Pleistocene Park thrill. He believes that bringing back the woolly mammoth to Eurasia and North America could help restore and preserve the delicate ecosystems there, perhaps even slowing global warming. The permafrost in polar regions is in danger of melting due to climate change, which would release a great deal of greenhouse gases, making the atmosphere even warmer. Large plant-eating animals help preserve the permafrost by digging up the snow in winter to get to the grass underneath. This removes the insulating snow and exposes the ground to the frigid air, keeping it frozen.

enzyme do its work, snipping out the defective sequence. Then they would use a genetically engineered virus to deliver and insert the normal DNA sequence to the gene, and then reintroduce the edited and healthy stem cells to the patient. Over time, scientists hope, the healthy stem cells will begin producing millions of healthy red blood cells.

GENE EDITING AND CANCER CELLS

Khalid Shah is the director of the Center for Stem Cell Therapeutics and Imaging at Brigham and Women's Hospital in Boston. He has figured out a way to use CRISPR to turn cancer cells into assassins that kill their own kind. Shah takes advantage of the tendency of metastasized cancer cells— those that escape a tumor and spread through the body—to return to the same tumor site, like homesick runaways coming home. Scientists believe the returning cancer cells may enhance tumor growth through the release of chemical signals.

Khalid Shah, director of the Center for Stem Cell Therapeutics and Imaging at Brigham and Women's Hospital in Boston, uses CRISPR technology to turn cancer cells into assassins that kill their own kind.

Z BABIES

In November 2018, a Chinese scientist stunned the scientific world when he announced that he had created the first babies genetically edited with CRISPR—twins, who had just been born. The scientist, He Jiankui, said a third genetically edited baby was on the way. Although other scientists have done gene-editing research on discarded human in vitro fertilization embryos, they were destroyed immediately afterward. This was the first time gene-edited embryos, created through in vitro fertilization, were used to create a pregnancy.

He said that his aim was to disable a gene called CCR5 so that the twin girls would be resistant to infection with HIV/AIDS. The change He made in the gene mimics a natural mutation that is relatively common in parts of northern Europe, but not in China. He said that the father of the girls had HIV, and he wanted to make sure that his children would not have it. But many critics think it was a reckless and terrible move. Where He sees a new form of medicine that can eliminate certain diseases, many others see it as medically risky.

"If true, this experiment is monstrous," Julian Savulescu, an ethics expert at the University of Oxford, told the BBC. "Gene editing itself is experimental and is still associated with . . . mutations, capable of causing genetic problems early and later in life, including the development of cancer." Even if the gene editing works as intended, people with a disabled CCR5 gene are at greater risk of becoming infected with other viruses or dying of influenza. Future generations could end up with these edited genes and their risks. Others said that much safer and more effective methods are available to prevent or treat HIV.

Shah and his colleagues started their experiments by removing cancerous tumor cells from a mouse. They used CRISPR to make the cells express a particular protein on the surface of its membrane. This protein attaches to "death receptors" on the surface of the target tumor cells, activating a cell-death program that kills the tumor cells. Shah injected the CRISPR-edited

It's unclear whether He's experiment is legal in China or whether he will be punished, but many scientists want to put a stop to creating pregnancies with gene-edited human embryos. Aside from the potential medical and health issues associated with gene-edited babies, people might use CRISPR technology to create "designer babies" with enhanced strength, perceived beauty, or other traits.

Biological researcher He Jiankui (*right*) guides a laboratory staff member at the Direct Genomics lab on August 4, 2016, in Shenzhen, Guangdong Province of China. Jiankui claimed to have created the world's first gene-edited twin baby girls "Lulu" and "Nana." They were said to possess genetic alterations that could protect them from HIV.

Jennifer Doudna, a professor at the University of California-Berkeley and one of the early CRISPR pioneers, told the *New York Times* that she was "horrified; I felt kind of physically sick," when she learned of He's experiment. In her book *A Crack in Creation: Gene Editing and the Unthinkable Power to Control Evolution*, Doudna writes that she was jolted awake by a dream in which Adolf Hitler (the leader of Nazi Germany in the 1930s and 1940s) asked her to describe "the uses and implications of this amazing technology you've developed." It made her realize that "the ability to refashion the human genome was a truly incredible power, one that could be devastating if it fell into the wrong hands."

cells into another mouse that had breast cancer that had spread to the brain. Sure enough, the assassin tumor cells homed in on the cancerous tumors in the brain, killing their target cells. The tumors shrank considerably. And 90 percent of the treated mice lived weeks or months following the treatment. The untreated mice, however, died quickly from the brain cancer.

Shah explained that bringing this therapy to the clinic for use in humans might require a slightly different approach. Using pre-edited assassin cells made from a donor and injecting them into another patient may prompt that patient's immune system to attack and kill the assassin cells. The alternative, which Shah has shown works in mice, is to engineer the patient's own cancer cells to become assassins. This would require removing a sample of cancer cells from the patient, editing them with CRISPR technology to express the molecule that binds to the death receptors on the target cancer cells, and injecting them back into the patient.

The disadvantage to this approach is that it takes three to four weeks to edit the cells and put them back into the patient, Shah said. Pre-edited cells made from a donor can be kept alive for a long time and can be available right away. Some cancer patients may not have the luxury of that much time. Whether the CRISPR-edited cells come from an outside donor or are the patient's own cells, Shah wanted to make sure that the assassin cells would not create problems of their own after killing the target tumor cells. They are, after all, still tumor cells. He and his team gave the assassin cells a "kill switch" so that giving the patient a drug would kill them after they had accomplished their task. Whether the gene-edited assassin cells will work in humans remains to be seen.

Shah is confident that cell-based therapies are the future of cancer treatment. He points to CAR-T cell therapy, a new way of harnessing the body's immune system to fight cancer. Doctors remove T cells from a patient and genetically engineer them to produce chimeric antigen receptors (CARs) on their surface. These receptors allow the T cells to recognize and kill cancer cells that have that antigen on their surface. In 2017 the FDA approved two CAR T-cell therapies using conventionally genetically engineered T cells. A clinical trial of CRISPR-engineered T cells is on the horizon.

Shah is excited about cell-based therapies for treating cancers. "Some drugs have really done wonders in some cancers," he acknowledged.

"For example, chemotherapy and radiation work well for breast cancer, but what we have not addressed is that there is a lot of toxicity [harmful side effects] in patients." And, he adds, brain, pancreatic, and some other cancers don't respond well to drug and radiation therapies. "I think that in the next ten years we are going to see a lot of cell-based therapies. If we have the power of gene editing cells, we should be able to tame them and ask them to do what we want."

OTHER PLAYERS

CRISPR is not the only game in town. One company, Sangamo Therapeutics, is betting on the success of zinc finger nucleases (ZFN). A nuclease is a scissorlike enzyme that can cut DNA. The company takes these naturally occurring proteins, which recognize and bind to specific DNA sequences, and engineer them to bind to any malfunctioning DNA sequence they choose. They can use these ZFNs to knock out or insert genes in the genome in a very specific way. "We cut your DNA, open it up, insert a gene, stitch it back up. Invisible mending," Sandy Macrae, president of Sangamo Therapeutics, told the Associated Press. "It becomes part of your DNA and is there for the rest of your life."

In 2017 a forty-four-year-old man named Brian Madeux got a ZFN that he and the scientists at Sangamo hope will improve the quality of his life. Madeux has Hunter's syndrome, a genetic disorder caused by a missing or defective enzyme. Madeux has joint stiffness, breathing problems, and developmental delays. He made scientific history as the first human being in history to receive a gene therapy injected directly into his body. The ZFN therapy most likely will not reverse the damage the disease has already done to his body, but it may halt its progression. Sangamo is recruiting patients to take part in similar studies to treat hemophilia, sickle cell disease, and other disorders.

SHINING A LIGHT ON NEUROSCIENCE

A new technique called optogenetics is taking neuroscience by storm. It uses a combination of gene therapy and light to control nerves. Optogenetics has the potential to cure blindness, relieve chronic pain, treat brain disorders, and more. Behind it is a humble single-celled alga called *Chlamydomonas reinhardtii*. The algae live in pond water and soil. Like plants, they make energy from sunlight. They have round bodies and two whiplike tails that propel them through water toward sources of light. They detect the light using something like primitive eyes, called eyespots, that contain light-sensitive proteins. One of these proteins is channelrhodopsin-2 (CR-2). It responds to blue light by pumping ions, or positively or negatively charged atoms, into nerve cells. CR-2 is what gives *C. reinhardtii* its superpower in neuroscience.

In humans and other animals, neurons communicate using a combination of electrical and

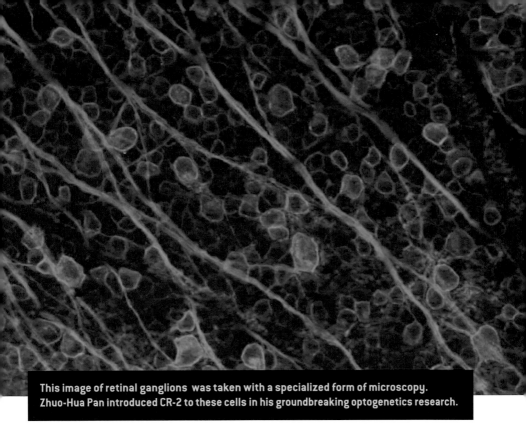

This image of retinal ganglions was taken with a specialized form of microscopy. Zhuo-Hua Pan introduced CR-2 to these cells in his groundbreaking optogenetics research.

chemical activity. Information flows from neuron to neuron across a small gap, or synapse. An electrical impulse causes the neuron to release chemicals, called neurotransmitters, which pass the message on to the next neuron. The usual trigger for animal neurons to transmit an electrical signal is the opening of ion channels in the neuron membrane. By inserting the *C. reinhardtii* gene coding for CR-2 into neurons, scientists can use light, instead of electricity, to open the ion channel.

Zhuo-Hua Pan, a vision scientist at Wayne State University in Detroit, Michigan, is among the pioneers of optogenetics. He was driven by a desire to cure blindness. The human retina is made of three layers. At the back of the eye are photoreceptors called rods and cones. Cones sense the colors red, green, and blue. Rods are color-blind, but they are more light sensitive than cones. A second layer is made of a network of interneurons. They pass information from the photoreceptors to the third layer of cells: the ganglions. It's up to the ganglions to relay this information to the brain. Pan said that some of the most common forms of blindness occur when rods

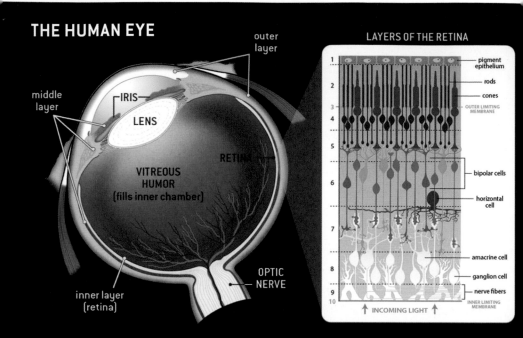

THE HUMAN EYE

outer layer

LAYERS OF THE RETINA

middle layer

IRIS

LENS

RETINA

VITREOUS HUMOR
(fills inner chamber)

OPTIC NERVE

inner layer
(retina)

1 — pigment epithelium
2 — rods
— cones
3 — OUTER LIMITING MEMBRANE
4
5
6 — bipolar cells
— horizontal cell
7
8 — amacrine cell
— ganglion cell
9 — nerve fibers
10 — INNER LIMITING MEMBRANE
↑ INCOMING LIGHT ↑

This infographic shows the basic parts of the human eye, including the iris, lens, retina, and vitreous humor. The inset at right shows the many layers of the retina itself. Zhuo-Hua Pan is researching techniques to restore vision by stimulating the neurons in the retina.

and cones die off. Then light information does not get passed to the other layers of the retina.

One approach to restoring vision is to surgically implant a device in each retina to electrically stimulate its neurons. But the devices could only hold sixty electrodes each, so it would create poor-quality images. Pan and his colleagues also worried that the technique would be too invasive and could cause long-term injury to the eye. "We thought making the second or third layers of cells in the retina light sensitive would be a more natural way to restore vision," Pan said, "by making new photoreceptors. The idea was quite simple, but the problem was how?"

Pan's team thought about inserting genes for light-sensitive proteins from human photoreceptors into the interneurons or ganglions, but it would be complicated and tricky. Human photoreceptors work along with several other proteins, so the team would have to insert several genes and get them all to function with one another. And then in 2003, Pan read a scholarly paper by a German group that described CR-2—the light-sensing protein in *C. reinhardtii.* "We were really excited, because it appeared that [CR-2] might be the ideal candidate for our study. Basically, we would just put one single gene into the cell, and it would respond to light."

Pan and his collaborators transferred the gene coding for CR-2 by using a harmless virus. Normally, viruses infect their hosts by inserting their genetic material into the nucleus of the host cell and forcing the cell to make copies of the virus. But this virus had been modified so that it would introduce the new CR-2 gene into the host cell without making the host cell make copies of the virus. (This method is the basis for many other kinds of gene editing.) By 2004 Pan used these viruses to insert the light-sensing gene into ganglion cells in a petri dish. It worked—the cells activated in response to light. Next, Pan injected the viruses carrying the CR-2 into the retinas of visually impaired mice. Again, it worked. The once-blind mice could detect light—but only very bright lights, since CR-2 is one thousand times less sensitive to light than cones.

By 2018 up to fifteen patients were in a clinical trial using Pan's technology. This is the first trial that involves putting nonhuman DNA into a human being. So far, none of the patients has had any negative side effects. Researchers report that patients can detect where in a room a window is. No one expects the therapy to restore vision completely, but it might improve vision so that visually impaired people can better navigate their world. Meanwhile, Pan is developing an opsin that is more light sensitive. "We are making a version of channelrhodopsin which can function under ambient [in surrounding] conditions," Pan said. "We've been able to achieve the visual acuity [clarity of vision] of about one-half that of a wild animal." Many wild animals have excellent vision, so for people who are blind and want to see, that sounds good.

LIGHT-POWERED BIOBOTS

Science fiction author Arthur C. Clarke had a pretty good track record for making scientific and technological predictions. In 1964 he said, "It will be possible . . . perhaps only 50 years from now for a man to conduct his business from Tahiti or Bali [in Indonesia] just as well as he could from London [in England]." By the end of the twentieth century, laptops and the internet made that prediction a reality.

Clarke also coined the term *biot* to describe biological robots made of biological and human-made materials. This is becoming a reality too. Rashid Bashir, head of bioengineering at the University of Illinois, is among the scientists fulfilling Clarke's prediction. Bashir has developed a class of walking "biobots" powered by rings of muscle cells that respond to light. Bashir and his team began by genetically engineering muscle cells with an opsin so that blue light stimulated the muscle cells to contract. He grew those muscle cells so that they formed a ring-shaped tissue. The team looped the rings around tiny 3D-printed flexible backbones and moved them daily to strengthen them. Shining a light on the tiny biobots—no larger than 0.8 inches (2 cm)—causes them to walk toward the light source.

Bashir envisions using biobots to design biological systems that could sense and respond to chemicals or other forces in the body. "We are still focusing on the basic design of the biobots," Bashir said, "but you can imagine a system where you could design blood vessels that have sensing capabilities so that if a blood clot forms, it could respond as pressure increases and make the clot disappear."

SHINING A LIGHT ON THE BRAIN

Around the same time, scientists at Stanford University in California and at other universities started to experiment with using light to control neurons. Karl Deisseroth, a neuroscientist and psychiatrist at Stanford, wanted to use optogenetics in brain cells. He thought that if technicians could target specific neurons—for example, those associated with memory or anxiety—they could create very precise maps of the brain's complex neural networks. They could also potentially treat neurological diseases.

Like Pan, Deisseroth and his colleagues introduced opsin DNA into rat neurons. They spliced the gene for CR-2 and a very specific kind of switch, or promoter, into the genetic material of a harmless virus that transferred the genes to the nucleus of the neurons. The promoter acted as a kind of password, ensuring that only certain kinds of neurons will make the newly encoded opsin proteins. Because the inside of any skull is very dark, Deisseroth's team had to figure out a way to deliver light to the targeted neurons. They solved that problem by inserting a thin fiber-optic wire (a cable that can carry light signals) directly into the rats' brains. Soon the team found that they could wake a sleeping mouse by delivering flashes of light into its brain through the wire. They could make a mouse run in circles on demand. More important, they used optogenetics to map the neural connections in mouse models for some brain disorders, including depression, schizophrenia, and autism.

PAIN MANAGEMENT

Chris Towne was a postdoctoral fellow in Deisseroth's lab. He is now senior director of gene therapy at Circuit Therapeutics, a company in Menlo Park, California, that aims to use optogenetics for human therapies. One of the most promising applications is pain relief.

In 2017 more than 115 people in the United States died every day from overdosing on opioids. This family of chemicals reduces pain, creates a feeling of euphoria, and slows breathing. Doctors prescribe opioids to treat severe pain, but these drugs can be extremely addictive and potentially deadly. Drug overdoses have become the leading cause of death of Americans under the age of fifty. Two-thirds of those deaths are from opioid overdoses. The US Drug Enforcement Administration tracks drug deaths and has stated in an official report that "overdose deaths, particularly from prescription drugs and heroin, have reached epidemic levels."

At least twenty-five million Americans suffer from chronic pain. The

VARIATIONS ON A THEME

One of the challenges of optogenetics is that it's not so easy to shine light where it's needed—especially if that place is deep within the brain. At this time, the only ways of delivering light to neurons in the brain is to use invasive optical fibers or wireless probes. Both can cause tissue damage and unwanted changes in behavior. But sound waves can easily pass through tissue to an intended target. Why not genetically modify cells to respond to sound waves instead? That's the idea behind a field that's still in its infancy: sonogenetics.

Sreekanth Chalasani and others at the Salk Institute in La Jolla, California, and at the University of California–San Diego have found a way to selectively activate brain cells using ultrasound. Ultrasound directs high-frequency sound waves toward an object to locate specific structures. For example, bats send sound waves to navigate their world. Physicians have used ultrasound for decades to look inside the body in a safe way. The technology is commonly used with pregnant women to see if the baby is developing normally.

The California researchers are using the roundworm, *Caenorhabditis elegans*, in their sonogenetics studies. *C. elegans* is a model organism for studying the neural development in animals. It's one of the simplest organisms with a nervous system, and scientists have mapped a complete diagram of the worm's 302 neurons. The scientists identified a neuron in the *C. elegans* nervous system that they predicted would make a worm reverse course as it was turning. They genetically modified that neuron to make it respond to ultrasound. As predicted, when the researchers triggered the neuron with a pulse of ultrasound, the worm changed the direction in which it had been moving. "The real prize will be to see whether this could work in a mammalian brain," Chalasani said. The next step: the mouse brain.

challenge for medicine and society is to curb drug abuse while helping people who are in pain. "In the eighty-thousand years that humans have been on earth, we've had four basic needs: to eat, find a partner, find

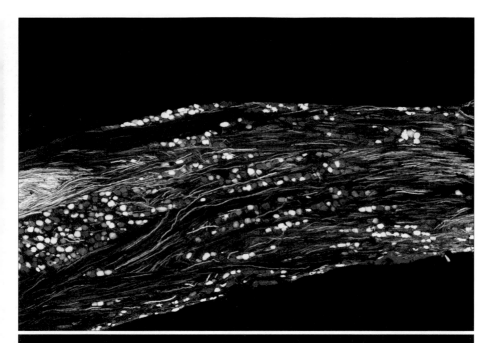

This specialized microscopy image shows another view of pain neurons and optogenetic proteins. Chris Towne's research focuses on using optogenetics to relieve pain in humans by turning off pain neurons with the use of light.

shelter, and avoid pain," said Towne. "In developed countries, at any rate, we have met all of those needs except one. Pain treatment is still very primitive; our drugs cause problems because they're nonspecific." Towne and others hope that optogenetics will provide a precisely targeted approach to pain management, relying on light's ability to pass through skin. "It's really nice, because you have nerve endings in the skin, and they're just waiting to be targeted with light."

Towne says the idea is to use a virus to deliver an opsin, coupled with promoter DNA, into the skin at the place where a patient experiences chronic pain. Only the pain neurons, not the touch or movement neurons, would be affected. Towne's treatment uses opsins that prevent neurons from firing. So a patient could wear a flexible LED patch that would lessen the pain neurons' ability to fire. The patient could use the patch to turn the light on or off at will, as they were experiencing pain. This approach is likely to work on pain neurons just under the skin. Chronic back pain lies deeper in the body, so it could be treated with a light-emitting implant that surgeons would place next to the spine. So far, Circuit Therapeutics has tested the therapy in mice and pigs. The company is working with the FDA to begin clinical trials in humans in the near future.

Towne also has his eye on using optogenetics to treat Parkinson's disease, a disorder that affects certain neurons in a specific area of the brain. People with Parkinson's often have tremors, slowed movement, stiff muscles, changes in their speech, or a combination of these conditions. One method of treating Parkinson's disease in people with severe tremors is to implant electrodes in specific areas deep within the brain to deliver electrical pulses there. "Parkinson's is a really nice first application of optogenetics in the brain," Towne said. "At the moment, you have 100,000 people walking around with deep brain stimulators." However, the stimulators do not deliver electrical pulses precisely, so patients often have side effects. For example, they have a lot of vocal problems, because that area of the brain is so close to the pathways that control voice. Towne says, "We'd like to use a similar approach, but with an optical fiber in the brain, so there will be a more targeted delivery." The optogenetic method would allow doctors to target only the neurons involved in Parkinson's disease. Researchers elsewhere have developed tiny devices that can be fully implanted in the brains of rodents and that are wirelessly powered by radio waves. This is an important step toward making the technology feasible for use in humans.

Towne and others envision a whole host of disorders that could be treatable with optogenetics. For example, Tobias Moser, a doctor and scientist at the Göttengen Institute for Auditory Neuroscience in Germany, has used optogenetics to bring hearing to deaf gerbils. Thousands of people with hearing impairments use cochlear implants, electrical devices placed in the part of the inner ear that receives sound in the form of vibrations. The implants allow them to hear and understand speech, but the devices are not ideal. Music often sounds strange, and it's hard to understand conversations in a loud room. Speaking to the *Scientist,* Moser compared the cochlea to a keyboard: "What you do with an electrical implant is actually you're not playing with your fingers but rather with your fist or your arm, because you're hitting many keys at a time."

Moser and his colleagues are working to put opsins into cochlear cells. Coupled with a light source to stimulate the cells, the technology would convert sound signals to light. The hope is that the cells could then be implanted into human ears. Sound would be vastly improved, enabling the person to play cochlear keys with fingers, not fists or arms, one note at a time.

MAGNETO

An alternative approach that borrows from optogenetics is magnetogenetics. Scientists at the University of Virginia engineered a gene to code for a protein that allows neurons to respond to magnetic fields. The scientists, Ali Deniz Güler and Michael Wheeler, named their new gene Magneto, after the Marvel Comics villain who can alter magnetic fields. This gene is no villain, however. The researchers inserted the gene into a set of neurons in mice associated with comfort or pleasure.

Mice with the Magneto gene loved to hang out in a chamber of their cage where lab technicians had turned on a magnetic field. When the technicians turned off the field, the mice didn't prefer that part of the cage. "The mice were hanging out in the magnetic chamber because they were experiencing some pleasure there, since we were . . . turning on the neurons that signal reward," said Michael Wheeler.

BETTER LIVING THROUGH CHEMISTRY

Yet another variation on the optogenetics theme is chemogenetics, using genes and chemicals to stimulate neurons. Scientists can engineer individual nerve cells in the brain so that they have chemical receptors

ION CHANNEL-LINKED RECEPTORS

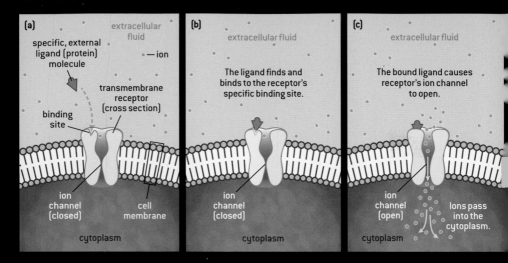

(a)
extracellular fluid

specific, external ligand (protein) molecule

— ion

transmembrane receptor (cross section)

binding site

ion channel (closed)

cell membrane

cytoplasm

(b)
extracellular fluid

The ligand finds and binds to the receptor's specific binding site.

ion channel (closed)

cytoplasm

(c)
extracellular fluid

The bound ligand causes receptor's ion channel to open.

ion channel (open)

Ions pass into the cytoplasm.

cytoplasm

Cell surface receptors of neurons act like gatekeepers, closed (a) until a specific protein, or ligand, binds to the receptor (b). This causes the receptor to open the gate, or channel, allowing extracellular ions to flood into the nerve cell (c).

that respond only to one specific drug. What's more, the drug will bind only to that receptor.

Mikhail Shapiro, a chemical engineer at California Institute of Technology in Pasadena, California, used this protocol to genetically modify neurons in the memory-forming cells of mice to respond to a drug designed in his lab. When the mice were given the drug, the memory-forming neurons were turned off. They temporarily couldn't form new memories.

Shapiro and his colleagues hope that chemogenetics might be used in other ways in the brain. For example, it may be useful in treating patients with epilepsy. Many people with severe epilepsy undergo surgery to cut out the parts of their brain that trigger seizures. Chemogenetics temporarily may be able to shut down, without surgery, the parts of the brain that trigger seizures.

DESIGNER BACTERIA

The human body has about thirty-nine trillion bacterial cells, or microbes. Most of which live in the gut, or digestive tract. By contrast, the body has about thirty trillion human cells, 84 percent of which are red blood cells. That's right—bacterial cells slightly outnumber human cells in our bodies. Together, the bacterial cells weigh about 3 to 5 pounds (1.3 to 2.3 kg) per person, and they help the body digest certain nutrients, produce vitamins, and crowd out potential disease-causing organisms. They help control the immune system, influencing whether we develop allergies or how well we fight off infectious diseases. Evidence suggests that an imbalance of "good" gut bacteria may play a role in obesity, depression, and autism, among other disorders. So while our microbiota—the collection of bacteria, fungi, and other microbes that live in our bodies—may not be official organs, they play a critical role in the health of the human body.

The human body has trillions of human cells, more than three-quarters of which are red blood cells (*above*). Yet bacterial cells far outnumber them and are responsible for keeping us healthy in a variety of ways.

Before we are born, we are sterile—our bodies have no beneficial microbes. Babies pick up bacteria from their mothers, other family members, and the environment. Over time, people develop their own distinctive community of microbes. One of the most important factors in developing healthy microbiota is diet. Justin Sonnenburg, associate professor of microbiology and immunology at the Stanford University School of Medicine, is an expert on gut microbes. "Nurturing our gut bacteria so that they produce the compounds that our bodies need is one of the most important choices we can make for our health," write Sonnenburg and his wife, Erica Sonnenburg, also a scientist at Stanford. What the gut bacteria like best are the complex carbohydrates found in fiber, vegetables, nuts, whole grains, and legumes.

Eating living bacteria as a health supplement or medicine is nothing new. Probiotics, for example, are easy to find in grocery stores and drugstores. They include dietary supplements and fermented foods such as yogurt and sauerkraut that contain naturally occurring microbes. But scientists at several synthetic biology companies want to take probiotics a step further. Scientists at Synlogic of Cambridge, Massachusetts, are engineering new probiotics, called Synthetic Biotic medicines, to treat specific diseases.

Paul Miller, chief scientific officer at Synlogic, explains the difference between genetic engineering and synthetic biology. Genetic engineering involves altering the genetic material of a cell, usually by transferring one gene from one cell to another. A classic example is genetically engineered insulin, a protein made in the pancreas that regulates blood sugar levels. People with Type 1 diabetes don't produce enough of the protein and must give themselves insulin injections. In the past, the only option was to use insulin made from ground-up pig or cow pancreas cells. Animal insulin is no longer available in the United States, so genetically engineered insulin is the only option.

Genetically engineered insulin is made by inserting the gene that codes for human insulin into a plasmid—a small circle of bacterial DNA. That plasmid is introduced into a new bacteria or yeast cell. When the cell divides, it produces insulin. The genetically modified bacteria or yeast cells are grown in large fermentation vats, so it is very easy to produce large quantities of insulin.

"Synthetic biology," Miller says, "takes it quite a bit further. We take the principles of electrical engineering and apply them to biology." Synthetic biologists aren't just copying and pasting DNA from one place to another. They figure out the function of specific DNA sequences (sometimes called BioBricks) and how they work. Then they put them together in new configurations to carry out new tasks. An electrical engineer puts capacitors, resistors, and diodes together in a certain way to build an electrical circuit. Miller and his colleagues engineer new genetic circuits by adding and subtracting BioBricks in a harmless strain of *E. coli* normally found in the human gut. The engineered bacteria are then made into pills for human consumption.

SYNTHETIC LIFE FROM SCRATCH

Biologist Craig Venter headed up the effort to map the entire human genome in 2001. Fifteen years later, in 2016, he announced that he and his team at the J. Craig Venter Institute had created a new form of life—from scratch. With just 473 genes, the new microbe, dubbed JCVI-syn3.0, has the smallest genome of any living thing. By comparison, humans have about 20,000 genes. Venter's goal was to create a stripped-down cell containing only the set of genetic instructions necessary for life—to convert nutrients to energy, to maintain the cell's structures, and to reproduce, for example—and no more. The role of 149 of the 473 genes is a mystery. Whether little JCVI-syn3.0 will lead to practical applications is unclear. But it may tell us something about what it means to be alive—and what is necessary for life.

JCVI-syn3.0 is not Venter's first effort in making synthetic life. In 2010 his team used the digital DNA code of the genome of *Mycoplasma mycoides*, a bacterium that infects cattle, to build a new genome in yeast cells. The new genome was identical to that of the original *M. mycoides*, with a few critical additions. To make clear that this genome was synthetic, the team inserted genetic watermarks—verbal messages coded into the cells using A, T, G, and C as their alphabet (much as a spy might write a message using a secret code). Among the watermarks were a website address for Venter's team and three quotations, including "See things not as they are, but as they might be."

The team inserted the newly built genome into a related

For example, one of Synlogic's first synthetic biotics, SYNB1020, is being tested in people with urea cycle disorder. Normally, the nitrogen we get from eating protein is converted to the chemical compound urea and then transferred naturally into our urine. People with the disorder can't process the nitrogen fast enough. It accumulates in the form of ammonia, a highly toxic chemical that can be deadly. SYNB1020 was designed to gobble up ammonia and turn it into arginine, a harmless amino acid.

bacterium that the researchers had stripped of its own genome. Some scientists hailed the resulting organism, JCVI-syn 1.0, as the first synthetic cell. Others said that this may have been an exaggeration, as the genome was made by copying an existing genome and not by designing a new one. But Venter's team had created, as he said in a TED Talk in 2010, "the first self-replicating species that we've had on the planet whose parent is a computer."

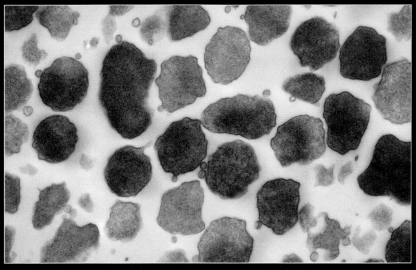

This colored electron micrograph shows *Mycoplasma mycoides* bacteria. This type of bacteria has no cell wall so it doesn't have a specific shape. These bacteria are also the smallest known bacteria and have a very small genome, so scientists can build new genomes with them fairly quickly.

A person with the disease could swallow a capsule containing about one hundred billion of the redesigned bacteria once a day. SYNB1020 doesn't take over the gut as other probiotics do. "It needs a specific medium to grow," said Elizabeth Wolffe, director of communications at Synlogic, "one that's not found at high levels in the gut." So the synthetic microbes would make their way only to the urea, mop up the extra ammonia, and get out of the body when the person urinates. Once out of the body, the synthetic microbes wouldn't be able to survive and wouldn't

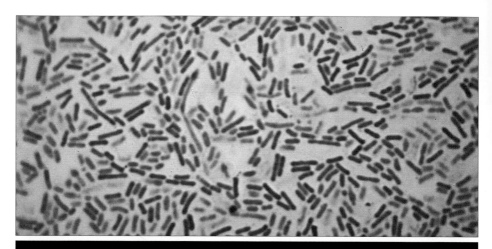

This micrograph from the Centers for Disease Control and Prevention shows *Bacteroides hypermegas* bacteria. Scientists are engineering different strains of *Bacteroides* as part of their microbiota research. They hope that beneficial microbes can help stimulate a patient's immune system as part of immunotherapy for cancers and autoimmune diseases.

pose a threat to the environment. "It's important to keep in mind," said Wolffe, "that we're generally doing things that you would normally do in your own cells."

"We don't invent new biochemistry, we look at what nature does and then ask, how can I incorporate that into my genetic circuit," said Miller.

ENGINEERING LONG-TERM RESIDENTS

Sonnenburg's lab at Stanford and a related company, Novome Biotechnologies, are developing ways to engineer therapeutic bacteria that can live permanently in the gut. Although we continue to gain or lose new microbes throughout our lives, it's very unpredictable. Once the gut microbiota is established, it can be tough for new microbes to settle in. Research that originated in Sonnenburg's lab and then at Novome may lead to a reliable way of introducing engineered bacteria to the gut. The key is seaweed—an ingredient relatively rare in American diets.

Scientists like working with *E. coli* because it is well understood. But if you want to engineer a microbe that will colonize, or make a new home, in the gut and give you the best therapeutic bang for your buck, *E. coli* is not necessarily your friend. "In terms of the makeup of the average healthy gut," says Liz Shepherd, cofounder of Novome and former postdoctoral fellow in Sonnenburg's lab, "it makes up about one percent of your gut microbes. Some people don't even have [permanent] *E. coli* in their microbiome [sometimes the term *microbiome* is used interchangeably with *microbiota.* It refers to the collection of genomes from all the microbes in the environment.]." But a different genus, *Bacteriodes,* makes up about one-half of the microbiota in the average American adult gut. And so Shepherd, Sonnenburg, and their colleagues went to the San Jose Wastewater Treatment Facility in central California. They collected sewage samples and screened them for *Bacteroides* strains that could digest a carbohydrate, called porphyran, found in the seaweed commonly used in sushi rolls and other Japanese foods. The porphyran-gobbling strains aren't common in American guts because most Americans didn't grow up eating seaweed.

The team found that when they gave the porphyran-digesting *Bacteriodes* to mice eating regular mouse chow, it didn't establish itself very well in the mouse guts. But when the mice were fed porphyran-rich diets, the seaweed-loving *Bacteroides* set up permanent residence in their guts. "You can imagine it was sort of like we were creating a new niche [for the porphyran-digesting *Bacteroides*], adding a new pocket for this bug to exist happily," Shepherd said. "We were able to increase or decrease the niche size [and switch] it up or down, depending on how much porphyran we gave the mice. It was very dependable."

The team found that the gene for porphyran digestion could be engineered into other strains of *Bacteroides.* With engineered strains of *Bacteroides* that can be reliably established in the gut, the possibilities for therapies are seemingly endless. "It's become very clear over the last ten years that gut microbes are not only wired to many aspects of our biology, but they are also very [adaptable]," Sonnenburg said. "A physician whose patient is about to begin immunotherapy for cancer may choose to administer a bacterial strain known to activate the immune system, for example.

ETHICAL ISSUES IN SYNTHETIC BIOLOGY

Synthetic biology offers the opportunity to transform medicine and chemical manufacturing, among other things. It might also be used to create, intentionally or accidentally, organisms that could be dangerous. And that has many people worried.

In June 2018, the National Academies of Sciences, Engineering, and Medicine issued a report detailing the ways that synthetic biology might be used to create bioweapons. If Venter's team could re-create *Mycoplasma mycoides* using easily obtainable chemicals, for example, could someone build a smallpox virus? In 1980 a worldwide vaccination campaign wiped out smallpox, an often-deadly contagious disease. The only remaining smallpox virus samples are in freezers in two secure locations in the United States and Russia. In January 2018, a Canadian scientist published a paper showing how he and his lab synthesized horsepox, a cousin of the smallpox virus. The scientist said he made the virus with the aim of creating a better vaccine. But critics said that his paper might have revealed to any bioterrorist the recipe for making smallpox.

Existing bacteria or viruses could be made even more dangerous by giving them resistance to antibiotics and vaccines or the ability to produce new toxins. Experts in national security and pandemics, or worldwide epidemics, at the Johns Hopkins Center for Health Security in Baltimore, Maryland, carried out a daylong tabletop exercise. The goal was to try to predict what would happen if a terrorist group released a new, deadly virus around the globe. The resulting fictional pandemic killed 150 million people within a year, causing social and economic chaos.

The panel made several recommendations to prevent or at least reduce the worst outcomes in such an event, including developing the capability of producing new vaccines more quickly and pioneering a strong, long-lasting global public health security system.

Conversely, a patient with an autoimmune disease may benefit from a different set of microbiota that can dial down an overactive immune response."

WHAT'S AHEAD

The possibilities for synthetic bacteria in medicine are seemingly endless. Scientists at MIT and the University of California—San Diego are experimenting with treating cancer with bacteria engineered to invade tumors and destroy cells from within. Bacteria grow very well inside tumors, which provide a safe harbor for the microbes and protect them from the body's immune system. The researchers engineered a strain of *Salmonella enterica* to produce an anticancer drug stored within the bacteria. They gave the drug to lab mice with cancerous tumors. They found that when the bacteria population within a tumor reached a certain level, the bacterial cells self-destructed and released their anticancer payload. The team then tested the engineered bacteria, along with traditional chemotherapy. The combination was a lot more effective than chemotherapy alone.

Other scientists are looking at ways to engineer microbes to produce pharmaceutical drugs. A team of scientists at the University of California—Berkeley engineered a yeast strain for a chemical to make artemisinin, a potent antimalarial drug. In nature, the wormwood plant naturally produces this chemical. But months or years of bad weather—increasingly common with climate change—could endanger the wormwood plant and threaten the global supply of artemisinin.

Some synthetic biologists are also experimenting with ways to produce proteins not found in nature. Scientists at the Scripps Research Institute in San Diego have produced two more amino acids besides DNA's familiar A, T, G, and C building blocks, dubbed X and Y. They engineered bacterial cells that would recognize the new amino acids and use them to make specific proteins. The researchers aren't sure if the proteins will be useful for treating humans. But the scientists may be able to engineer the synthetic microbes to do other helpful things, such as eat up cancer cells.

CAREERS IN BIOMEDICAL ENGINEERING

G ilda Barabino, professor of biomedical and chemical engineering, says that some students are naturally inclined to become engineers because they're tinkerers—they like to take things apart and put them back together again. Does that sound like you? If you like science, math, and problem-solving, biomedical engineering just might be the career for you. According to the US Bureau of Labor Statistics projections, employment of biomedical engineers will grow 7 percent from 2016 to 2026. That's about average for all occupations, so it's a promising field.

The minimum education students need to prepare for a career in biomedical engineering is a bachelor's degree. Colleges and universities offer undergraduate degrees in biomedical engineering and bioengineering. But if you are interested in doing your own original research, you will need to pursue a PhD after earning your bachelor's degree. If you are interested in the

PhD route, start by earning your bachelor's degree in an established field such as biology, physics, chemistry, computer science, or engineering.

Think about a problem you want to solve, Barabino tells students. Think about something that's important to you. "Young people usually have something in mind: 'I want to save the world. I want to make a difference.' I tell them to think about engineering as a strategy to do that. What you get out of engineering are a set of tools, a way of thinking and problem solving. But I would posit that you don't have to see yourself as a tinkerer to be an engineer," Barabino says. "I think there's a little bit of an engineer in everybody. It's curiosity! Everybody wants to know how things work."

In college Barabino studied chemistry, with an eye to going to medical school. She decided she was too squeamish to be a doctor, but she still wanted to help people. "I decided that engineering should allow me to apply some basic fundamental concepts to medicine," she said. So she earned her PhD in chemical engineering. Her initial focus was on fluid mechanics and blood flow, especially as it applied to the abnormal blood flow in sickle cell disease.

Like Barabino, Gordana Vunjak-Novakovic initially wanted to study medicine, but "decided I didn't have the stomach for it." She loved music and writing but felt she lacked the talent. She decided to study chemical engineering, "because my dad was an engineer." After graduate school, she took a serendipitous path, exploring several different areas of research until she discovered a new field that clicked with her—tissue engineering. "I found a way to circle back to medicine in a different way," she said.

Kacey Ronaldson, a postdoctoral fellow in Vunjak-Novakovic's lab, also thought she wanted to be a doctor. In college her first job was working in ambulances—and that was enough to convince her that she really didn't want to be a doctor. "I took an internship in materials engineering," she said, "and that kind of clicked. I still wanted to help people, and biomedical engineering seemed to be a good way to do that."

DISCOVER YOUR PASSION

"I think what's important is that you try out different things early on," said Karen Echeverri, who grew up in Ireland and was the only child in her family to finish her university education. She initially studied physics, "but that didn't motivate me very well," so she ended up getting a dual degree in biochemistry and microbiology. As an undergraduate and then as a graduate student, she worked in several labs across Europe, studying yeast and drosophila, or fruit flies. Nothing really clicked until she heard a seminar by Elly Tanaka, the woman who would become her PhD mentor, and "completely fell in love with regeneration. So I had quite a circuitous route to getting my PhD! I think that for young people it's really important to find something you're passionate about. Don't let failure get you down— failing at things, or finding things you don't like, is the path to finding what you are passionate about."

Abidemi Bolu Ajiboye earned a dual bachelor of science degree in biomedical and electrical engineering, with a minor in computer science.

He says that students interested in the field should have a fundamental understanding of the sciences and mathematics. "But then I'd also say, 'Get out of the classroom and pursue something you really enjoy . . . really learn how to solve problems, because the people who are working on these neural engineering problems have diverse backgrounds. The one common thread is that they all know how to solve really hard problems. It creates a mentality for trying to not only come up with novel questions, but also having the perseverance to solve them."

Jeffrey Capadona also encourages students to explore new areas of interest. "Don't be afraid to reach out to volunteer and learn," he said. "We take high school and college students [into our lab]; we don't care if they don't have a strong background yet. We are here to teach and inspire." Suraj Srinivasan, a high school student at Strongsville (Ohio) High School, worked in Capadona's lab. He took first place in the prestigious Intel International Science and Engineering Fair in 2017. "He's getting scholarships for wherever he wants to go now," Capadona said, "and all because he reached out to us, and was willing to learn and engage."

Capadona, who majored in chemistry and minored in mathematics in college, grew up thinking he wanted to become a doctor. He hurt his back playing on his college baseball team, so he was sidelined his senior year. "I was kind of devastated by that," he admitted. Orthopedic surgeons said that they could do surgery on his back, but that by his forties, he probably

Biomedical engineer Abidemi Bolu Ajiboye says that a passion for problem-solving in the real world is a great way to prepare for a career in his field. His goal in the research he does is to create BCI systems that allow people to work easily and naturally with artificial limbs and other assistive technologies.

would be arthritically crippled. "I was frustrated that the doctors were so limited in what they could do, so I was inspired to looking into new technologies. At the time I didn't even know that biomedical engineering as a field existed."

After getting his PhD in chemistry at Georgia Tech, where he worked on creating new orthopedic materials, Case Western Reserve recruited him. They needed somebody with a background in chemistry to make materials for brain implants. Capadona jumped at the chance: "I was like, wow, that's so cool—I'm a chemist and I get to do brain surgery!"

SCIENTISTS AS DETECTIVES

"This will probably sound corny, but one of the first careers I got excited about was being a detective," Liz Shepherd said. "I went to a police station that opened in my town when I was about seven, and I remember going to the detective unit and thinking that looking for clues and solving a mystery was so cool." About that time, scientists were beginning to sequence the human genome, and her father encouraged her to read books on genetics. "Although I didn't realize it at the time, I think that was how I transferred my interest from detective clue searching to biological clue searching." She studied microbiology in college. She also was in a summer competition sponsored by MIT for students to complete a project in synthetic biology. "It was such a cool demonstration of how you could engineer biology," Shepherd said.

Paul Miller was interested in science and math in high school and thought he might become a doctor. But he took a biochemistry class in college where the professor emphasized the nature of biochemical pathways in diseases. What would happen if cells were unable to produce the enzyme responsible for converting ammonia into urea, for example?

"That class caused me to switch my focus," Miller said, who went on to earn his PhD in microbiology. He initially focused on discovering new antibiotics—"trying to figure out how to kill bacteria"—and now he's creating new, beneficial microbes.

Elizabeth Wolffe's early interests were Egyptology and writing, but her father encouraged her to pursue a career in science. She became enamored with biology, because it seemed that so much still needed to be discovered. "I thought about medicine, but my stomach wasn't strong enough," she said. She studied microbiology and cell biology, and she "never regretted it for an instant. This is really the golden age of biology," she added.

PERSEVERANCE PAYS

Zhuo-Hua Pan, born in China, was in third grade when the nation's premier, Mao Zedong, launched what became known as the Cultural Revolution. Believing that China was drifting too far away from its Communist beliefs, he set out to destroy all aspects of Chinese culture that didn't support communism. Intellectuals and people identified as "class enemies" were persecuted or killed. Mao shut down many schools, and educated young people from the cities were sent to the countryside to do hard labor on farms.

Pan, whose father was a high school mathematics teacher, was allowed to finish middle school, but high school was out of the question. Instead, young Pan, who dreamed of becoming a mathematician like his father, was sent to work on the farms for three years. Eventually, he attended high school but then had to work on the farms for another three years. "Even in the countryside," Pan said, "I spent my time reading books about mathematics. I never dreamed I could go to college, but I thought that someday, if I got the chance, I would be prepared."

As a young man growing up in China, Zhuo-Hua Pan never dreamed he would be able to attend college. Today he is one of the pioneers of the growing field of optogenetics, driven by a desire to cure blindness.

Pan's focus paid off. After Mao died in 1976, political reform came to China, and students were allowed to take college entrance exams. He scored very well on both mathematics and physics. Much to his dismay, he was compelled to major in physics—a field he found "not very interesting." Knowing that he would never become a mathematician, Pan earned a master's degree in biophysics at a Chinese university. He came to the United States to further his education, and his interest in the retina was cemented when he studied with a retina researcher at State University of New York—Buffalo for his PhD.

Chris Towne always thought he'd be a lawyer. As a kid growing up in Australia, one of his favorite movies was the military legal drama *A Few Good Men*. When he went to college, he took some biology classes. "Evolution was just the greatest concept—I was blown away!" But he thought his law lectures were boring. "I was really intrigued by the scientific method," Towne said. "I wanted to make a real change, and coming up with an idea that nobody ever had before was just so exciting to me." He got an undergraduate degree in biotechnology and went to Switzerland to earn his PhD, working in a lab that studied gene therapy.

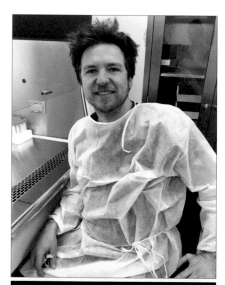

Chris Towne focuses his gene therapy research on pain relief. He is motivated by a desire to make innovations that will help people live better lives, free from suffering.

"I'm not that interested in discovering a new pathway in a cell," Towne said. "I'd rather come up with creative methods of helping an animal live longer, remove their pain or relieve their depression."

Khalid Shah remembers being a very curious boy when he was young. Shah, who grew up in Kashmir, remembers that when he and his classmates played cricket in school, he created balls for the game from the knots in trees. "You had to be innovative!" he said. The one trait, he says, that he sees in people who become successful scientists is a curious mind. He mentors young scientists at every level of education, noting that one of the coauthors on a recent paper was a high school student.

Like so many researchers in biomedical engineering, Khalid Shah of Brigham and Women's Hospital in Boston sees curiosity as a key trait in the people who are successful in his field.

No single path leads to a career in biomedical engineering—there are many. But it's easy to detect a common theme among the scientists who are attracted to the field. They are curious, persistent, and open to new ideas. They are often idealistic, holding firm to a dream that they can truly make their world a better place.

As Vunjak-Novakovic put it, "Aim high. Think big. Dream big dreams. Because you don't want to work on something that will only incrementally change things. Find something that you love to do. And never give up . . . you need to be very persistent, as stubborn as a mule, in order to succeed." Career options have changed greatly over the past ten years, she said. You could choose from just a few options: doctor, scientist, or engineer. She says, "Today, you can design your professional life. I think this new generation is great and brave, and they should not be scared of exploring something completely unconventional. . . . In ten or twenty years, we cannot predict how the world will look. You need to be smart and flexible, be brave and give yourself permission to explore something unique. Today is the best time to be in the biomedical sciences and engineering."

GLOSSARY

algae: plural of alga, a simple nonflowing plant of a large group that includes seaweeds and many single-celled forms

algorithm: a process or set of rules to be followed in calculations or other problem-solving operations

ambient: relating to the immediate surroundings of something

antigen: a foreign substance that induces an immune response in the body

artificial intelligence: computer systems able to perform tasks that normally require human intelligence, such as visual perception and decision-making

bacteria: a microscopic single-celled organism lacking a nucleus

bioengineering: the application of engineering principles, practices, and technologies to the fields of medicine and biology

brain-computer interface (BCI): a collaboration between a brain and a computer that enables signals from the brain to direct some external activity, such as control, a computer cursor, or a prosthetic limb

bronchi: plural form of bronchus, any of the major air passages of the lungs that branch out from the windpipe

cartilage: firm but flexible connective tissue found in various forms throughout the body, including the surfaces of joints

chemotherapy: using chemical substances to treat disease

chondrocyte: a cartilage cell

chromosome: DNA-containing structures of cellular organisms located in the nucleus of organisms

clone: an individual grown from a single body cell of its parent and having the same genes as its parent

cochlear: relating to the cochlea, a spiral-shaped cavity of the inner ear containing the nerve endings that transmit sound vibrations from the middle ear to the auditory nerve

collagen: the main structural protein found in skin and connective tissues

culture: as in a lab or cellular culture of living cells in a special liquid or jellylike nutrient preparation

deoxyribonucleic acid (DNA): a self-replicating molecule present in nearly all living organisms as the main part of chromosomes. It is the carrier of genetic information.

dialysis: in medicine, the purification of blood as a substitute for the normal function of the kidney

electrode: a conductor used to establish electrical contact with a nonmetallic part of a circuit

electroencephalograph (EEG): a machine used for electroencephalography, the measurement of electrical activity in different parts of the brain and the recording of such activity

embryonic: relating to the embryo, an unborn or unhatched living thing in the process of development

epithelial: relating to the thin tissue forming the outer layer of a body's surface and lining the gut and other hollow structures

ethics: the moral principles that govern the behavior of a person or a group of people

extracellular matrix (ECM): a collection of molecules secreted by cells that provides structural and biochemical support to the surrounding cells

fetal: of, relating to, or being a fetus (a developing human from usually two months after conception to birth)

ganglion: a structure containing a number of nerve cell bodies, typically linked by synapses

genome: the complete set of genes or genetic material present in a cell or organism

growth factor: a substance, such as a vitamin or hormone, which is required for the stimulation of growth in living cells

hydrogel: a biomaterial made up of a network of polymer chains that are highly absorbent and as flexible as natural tissue

immune system: a collection of cells, tissues, and molecules that protect the body from foreign substances, cells, and tissues

in vitro: a process taking place in a test tube, culture dish, or elsewhere outside of a living organism

in vivo: a process taking place in a living organism

microbiome: the collective genomes of microbes inhabiting a particular environment and especially the human body

microbiota: the collection of organisms (such as bacteria, fungi, and viruses) inhabiting a particular environment, especially the human body

multipotent: (of a cell) having the ability to differentiate to a limited number of cell types or into closely related families of cells

opioid: a class of drugs related to opium that includes the illegal drug heroin as well as pain relievers available legally by prescription

optogenetics: a technique in neuroscience in which genes for light-sensitive proteins are introduced into specific types of neurons to monitor, control their activity precisely with light signals, or both

ovary: one of the typically paired female reproductive organs that produce eggs, and in vertebrates, female sex hormones

photoreceptor: a structure in a living organism, especially a sensory cell or sense organ, that responds to light falling on it

plasmid: a segment of DNA, independent of the chromosomes and capable of replication, occurring in bacteria and yeast; often used in recombinant DNA procedures

pluripotent: (of a cell) having the ability to develop into any type of cell or tissue except those that form a placenta or embryo. Induced pluripotent stem cells (iPS) are those that are engineered directly from adult stem cells.

polymer: a chemical compound or mixture of compounds consisting essentially of repeating structural units

precursor: a substance, cell, or cellular component from which another substance, cell, or cellular component is formed

promoter: a binding site in a DNA chain that helps start the process of transcribing the DNA into an RNA molecule, the first step in making a protein

prosthesis: an artificial body part, such as a leg or arm

radiation: in medicine, the treatment of disease, especially cancer, using X-rays or similar forms of radiation

regenerate: to regrow new tissue to replace lost or injured tissue

retina: the sensory membrane that lines the eye, functioning as the immediate instrument of vision by receiving the image formed by the lens, converting it into chemical and electrical signals, and sending it to the brain by way of the optic nerve

ribonucleic acid (RNA): a molecule found in the cytoplasm of cells, involved in protein synthesis

scaffold: a structure of artificial or natural materials on which tissue is grown to mimic a biological process outside the body or to replace a diseased or damaged tissue inside the body

stem cell: an unspecialized cell that gives rise to different types of cells

symbiosis: the interaction between two different organisms living in close physical association, typically to the advantage of both

synthetic biology: the application of computer science techniques to create artificial biological systems

T cell: a cell that circulates in the blood and orchestrates the immune system's response to infected or cancer cells

telepathy: the communication of thoughts or ideas by means other than the known senses

3D printing: the action or process of making a physical object from a three-dimensional digital model, typically by laying down many thin layers of a material in succession

tremor: in medicine, an involuntary quivering movement

ultrasound: sound or other vibrations at the ultrasonic frequency, often used in medical imaging

virus: an infective agent that typically consists of an RNA or DNA molecule in a protein coat. It is too small to see under a light microscope and is able to multiply only within the living cells of a host.

zinc finger nuclease (ZFN): a man-made enzyme engineered to target and cut specific regions of DNA molecules

SOURCE NOTES

5   Walt Whitman, "Song of Myself," *Leaves of Grass: The First (1855) Edition*, ed.
        Malcolm Cowley, (New York: Penguin Classics, 1961) 29.

14   Hermes Taylor-Weiner and Joshua Graff Zivin, "Medicine's Wild West—
        Unlicensed Stem-Cell Clinics in the United States," *New England Journal of
        Medicine* 373 (2015): 985–987, https://www.nejm.org/doi/full/10.1056/
        NEJMp1504560/.

17   Karen Echeverri, personal communication with the author, March 13, 2018.

17   Echeverri.

20   Matthew Shaer, "Need a New Organ? Surgeon Anthony Atala Sees a Future
        Where You Can Simply Print It Out," *Smithsonian Magazine*, December 2016,
        https://www.smithsonianmag.com/innovation/miracle-maker-
        anthony-atala-winner-smithsonian-ingenuity-awards-2016-life-
        sciences-180961121/.

21   Stefanie Dion Jones, "Gratitude: Lucas Massella," *UConn Magazine*, Spring
        2014, 12–13.

23   Gilda Barabino, personal communication with the author, November 20,
        2017.

24   Barabino.

24   Barabino.

25   Gordana Vunjak-Novakovic, personal communication with the author,
        January 11, 2018.

25   Vunjak-Novakovic.

25, 27 Vunjak-Novakovic.

30   "Tissue Engineering: Personalized Medicine of the Future, Kacey
        Ronaldson, TEDxThunderBay," YouTube video, 14:01, posted by TEDx Talks,
        July 19, 2016, https://www.youtube.com/watch?v=hWr9FdpLxrg.

30–31   Kacey Ronaldson, personal communication with the author, January 22,
        2018.

31   Ronaldson.

35   A. Bolu Ajiboye, personal communication with the author, March 29, 2018.

36   Ajiboye.

36   "Man with Quadriplegia Employs Injury Bridging Technologies to Move
        Again—Just by Thinking," Case Western Reserve Daily, March 28, 2017,
        https://thedaily.case.edu/man-quadriplegia-employs-injury-bridging
        -technologies-move-just-thinking/.

37   Ajiboye, personal communication.

38   "Enabling Amputees to Discern Light Touch to Intense Pressure," YouTube Video, 3:25, posted by Case Western Reserve University, October 26, 2016, https://www.youtube.com/watch?v=JOyUhd1pj_Q.

38   Jeffrey Capadona, personal communication with the author, April 6, 2018.

38   Capadona.

40   *Batman Forever* (Quotes), IMDb, 1995, accessed May 9, 2019, https://www.imdb.com/title/tt0112462/quotes/.

40   Sarah Marsh, "Neurotechnology, Elon Musk and the Goal of Human Enhancement," *Guardian* (US edition), January 1, 2018, https://www.theguardian.com/technology/2018/jan/01/elon-musk-neurotechnology-human-enhancement-brain-computer-interfaces.

41   "Brainiac Says We'll All Be Part of the 'Brain-Net' Someday," *NBC News*, last modified April 3, 2014, https://www.nbcnews.com/science/science-news/brainiac-says-well-all-be-part-brain-net-someday-n70236.

41   "A Conversation with Elon Musk, CEO of Tesla Inc. at World Government Summit 2017 Dubai," YouTube video, 1:08:14, posted by *Khaleeg Times*, February 13, 2017, https://www.youtube.com/watch?v=jBuLgBX2bKQ.

41   "Conversation with Elon Musk."

42   Elon Musk, "Creating a Neural Lace Is the Thing That Really Matters for Humanity to Achieve Symbiosis with Machines," Twitter, June 4, 2016, https://twitter.com/elonmusk/status/739006012749799424.

50   "He Jiankui Defends 'World's First Gene-Edited Babies,'" *BBC News*, November 28, 2018, https://www.bbc.com/news/world-asia-china-46368731.

51   Pam Belluck, "How to Stop Rogue Gene-Editing of Human Embryos?," *New York Times*, January 23, 2019, https://www.nytimes.com/2019/01/23/health/gene-editing-babies-crispr.html.

51   Jennifer Doudna, *A Crack in Creation: Gene Editing and the Unthinkable Power to Control Evolution* (New York: Houghton Mifflin Harcourt, 2017), 199.

52–53 Khalid Shah, personal communication with the author, July 19, 2018.

53   Marilynn Marchione, "U.S. Scientists Try 1st Gene Editing in the Body," AP News, November 15, 2017, https://apnews.com/4ae98919b52e43d8a8960e0e260feb0a/AP-Exclusive:-US-scientists-try-1st-gene-editing-in-the-body.

56   Zhuo-Hua Pan, personal communication with the author, May 17, 2018.

57   Pan.

57 Pan.

58 Rashid Bashir, personal communication with the author, October 27, 2017.

59 *2015 National Drug Threat Assessment Summary*, Drug Enforcement
    Administration, October 2015, https://www.dea.gov/sites/default
    /files/2018-07/2015%20NDTA%20Report.pdf.

60 Salk Institute, "Controlling Brain Cells with Sound Waves," ScienceDaily,
    September 15, 2015, https://www.sciencedaily.com/releases/2015
    /09/150915135412.htm.

60–61 Chris Towne, personal communication with the author, July 18, 2018.

61 Towne.

62 Towne.

63 Shawna Williams, "Optogenetic Therapies Move Closer to Clinical Use,"
    Scientist, November 16, 2017, https://www.the-scientist.com/news
    -opinion/optogenetic-therapies-move-closer-to-clinical-use-30611.

63 Chris Higgins, "Arthur C. Clarke Predicts the Future in 1964," Mental Floss,
    June 7, 2015, http://mentalfloss.com/article/57157/arthur-c-clarke
    -predicts-future-1964.

63 University of Virginia, "UVA Scientists Use Synthetic Gene and Magnets to
    Alter Behavior of Mice, Fish," EurekaAlert!, March 7, 2016, https://
    www.eurekalert.org/pub_releases/2016-03/uov-usu030116.php.

66 Justin Sonnenburg and Erica Sonnenburg, *The Good Gut: Taking Control of
    Your Weight, Your Mood, and Your Long-Term Health,* (New York: Penguin,
    2015), 1.

67 Paul Miller, personal communication with the author, April 17, 2018.

69–70 Elizabeth Wolffe, personal communication with the author, April 17, 2018.

68 Craig Venter, "Watch Me Unveil 'Synthetic Life,'" TED in the Field, May 2010,
    https://www.ted.com/talks/craig_venter_unveils_synthetic_life.

69 Venter.

70 Miller, personal communication.

71 Liz Shepherd, personal communication with the author, May 18, 2018.

71 Shepherd, personal communication.

71, 73 Krista Conger, "Scientists Use Dietary Seaweed to Manipulate Gut Bacteria
    in Mice," Stanford Medical Center press release, May 9, 2018, https://
    med.stanford.edu/news/all-news/2018/05/scientists-use-dietary
    -seaweed-to-manipulate-gut-bacteria.html.

75 Barabino, personal communication.

75 Barabino.

76   Vunjak-Novakovic, personal communication.

76   Ronaldson, personal communication.

76   Echeverri, personal communication.

77   Ajiboye, personal communication.

77   Capadona, personal communication.

77   Capadona.

78   Capadona.

78   Shepherd, personal communication.

78   Miller, personal communication.

79   Wolffe, personal communication.

79–80 Pan, personal communication.

80   Pan.

80   Pan.

80   Towne, personal communication.

81   Shah, personal communication.

81   Vunjak-Novakovic, personal communication.

SELECTED BIBLIOGRAPHY

Church, George, and Ed Regis. *Renegesis: How Synthetic Biology Will Reinvent Nature and Ourselves.* New York: Basic Books, 2012.

Enriquez, Juan, and Steve Gullans. *Evolving Ourselves: Redesigning the Future of Humanity—One Gene at a Time.* New York: Current, 2016.

Mukherjee, Siddhartha. *The Gene: An Intimate History.* New York: Scribner, 2016.

Piore, Adam. *The Body Builders: Inside the Science of the Engineered Human.* New York: HarperCollins, 2017.

Platoni, Kara. *We Have the Technology: How Biohackers, Foodies, Physicians, & Scientists Are Transforming Human Perception, One Sense at a Time.* New York: Basic Books, 2015.

Yong, Ed. *I Contain Multitudes: The Microbes within Us and a Grander View of Life.* New York: HarperCollins, 2016.

FURTHER INFORMATION

Books

Doudna, Jennifer A., and Samuel H. Sternberg. *A Crack in Creation: Gene Editing and the Unthinkable Power to Control Evolution.* New York: Houghton Mifflin Harcourt, 2017.

Hirsch, Rebecca E. *De-Extinction: The Science of Bringing Lost Species Back to Life.* Minneapolis: Twenty-First Century Books, 2017.

———. *The Human Microbiome: The Germs That Keep You Healthy.* Minneapolis: Twenty-First Century Books, 2017.

Knight, Rob, and Brendan Buhler. *Follow Your Gut: The Enormous Impact of Tiny Microbes.* New York: TED Books, 2015.

Nicolelis, Miguel. *Beyond Boundaries: The New Neuroscience of Connecting Brains with Machines—and How It Will Change Our Lives.* New York: Times Books, 2011.

Videos

"The Augmented Human Being," YouTube video, 49:42. Posted by the Artificial Intelligence Channel, August 28, 2017. https://www.youtube.com /watch?v=ZqgeRxeglXw. George Church, professor of genetics at Harvard Medical School and professor of health sciences and technology at Harvard and MIT, explains how synthetic biology someday might radically change human beings.

How to Build a Beating Heart. DVD. New York: National Geographic, 2011. National Geographic explores the science of tissue engineering and tracks how scientists are harnessing the body's natural powers to grow skin, muscle, and vital organs—even hearts.

"The Mission to Resurrect the Woolly Mammoth." YouTube video, 22:02. Posted by Motherboard, April 8, 2015. https://www.youtube.com/watch?v=xmlpSOHc5A4. Motherboard describes the practice of cloning beloved pet dogs and asks if cloning extinct animals, including the woolly mammoth, is the next logical step.

"Printing a Human Kidney." Anthony Atala, TED2011, March 2011, 16:48. https:// www.ted.com/talks/anthony_atala_printing_a_human_kidney. Anthony Atala, professor and director of the Wake Forest Institute for Regenerative Medicine at Wake Forest School of Medicine in North Carolina, describes the process of using a 3D printer to make artificial human kidneys.

Websites

Brain Power: Bright Ideas and Smart Tools for Neuroengineering
https://www.nsf.gov/eng/special/brainpower/
This interesting and accessible government website focuses on the ways in which scientists and engineers are exploring the nervous system and developing exciting new opportunities and technologies.

Genetic Literacy Project
https://geneticliteracyproject.org
The Genetic Literacy Project explores innovations in human genetics and biotechnology. Topics addressed are CRISPR and gene editing, gene therapy, stem cell research, synthetic biology, and more.

Human Microbiome Project
https://commonfund.nih.gov/hmp
The Common Fund's Human Microbiome Project develops research resources to study the microbial communities that live in and on our bodies and the roles they play in human health and disease.

StemBook
https://www.stembook.org
StemBook is a collection of content covering a range of topics related to stem cell biology written by top researchers in the field.

Tissue Engineering and Regenerative Medicine
https://www.nibib.nih.gov/science-education/science-topics/tissue-engineering-and-regenerative-medicine
This US government website provides a general overview of tissue engineering and regenerative medicine, with a glossary and resource links.

What Are Genome Editing and CRISPR-Cas9?
https://ghr.nlm.nih.gov/primer/genomicresearch/genomeediting
This National Library of Medicine website explains gene editing and provides links to a series of fact sheets and other websites related to gene editing.

INDEX

PHOTO ACKNOWLEDGMENTS

Image credits: Design elements: Anna Rassadnikova/Shutterstock.com. Content: © Matjaz Kacicnik/Universität Basel, p. 5; John Cancalosi/Alamy Stock Photo, p. 8 (top); Andrea Izzotti/Alamy Stock Photo, p. 8 (bottom); Giovanni Cancemi/Shutterstock.com, p. 10; Juan Gaertner/Shutterstock. com, p. 11; Prime Minister's Office, Government of India/Wikimedia Commons (India (GODL)), p. 12; Laura Westlund/Independent Picture Service, pp. 13, 45, 46, 56, 64; National Toxicology Program/Department of Health and Human Services/Wikimedia Commons (Public Domain), p. 15; Jim Cumming/Alamy Stock Photo, p. 16; Steve Jurvetson/Wikimedia Commons (CC BY 2.0), p. 19; © Kevin Yueh-Hsun Yang, Ph.D., p. 24; NIAID/ flickr (CC BY 2.0), p. 29; AF archive/Alamy Stock Photo, p. 33; ullstein bild/ Getty Images, p. 34; © A. Bolu Ajiboye, PhD, pp. 37, 77; RGR Collection/ Alamy Stock Photo, p. 42; © Dr. Khalid Shah MS,Ph.D, pp. 49, 81; VCG/ VCG/Getty Images, p. 51; Dr. Zhuo-Hua Pan, p. 55; © Christopher Towne, pp. 61, 80, BSIP/UIG/Getty Images, p. 66; Thomas Deerinck, NCMIR/ Science Source, p. 69; Smith Collection/Gado/Getty Images, p. 70; Courtesy of Gilda A. Barabino, Ph.D, p. 75; Courtesy Dr. Zhuo-Hua Pan, p. 79.

Cover: Kotkoa/Shutterstock.com; Anna Rassadnikova/Shutterstock.com; Andrii Vodolazhskyi/Shutterstock.com.

ABOUT THE AUTHOR

Sara Latta is the author of more than thirty nonfiction and science books for children and young adults. Recent titles include *Smash! Exploring the Mysteries of the Universe with the Large Hadron Collider,* and *Black Holes: The Weird Science of the Most Mysterious Objects in the Universe.* A would-be scientist, she earned her master's degree in immunology from the University of Chicago before deciding that she'd rather write about science instead.